Like all fine writers, Dhivan Thomas Jones makes complex ideas simple and subtle truths compelling. The Buddha considered conditionality the heart of his message and fathoming it the key to a happy, creative and fulfilling life. This excellent book teases out his meaning and makes you want to start putting it into practice right away.

Vishvapani Blomfield, author of
Gautama Buddha: the Life and Teachings of the Awakened One

Clearly and intelligently written, *This Being, That Becomes* carries a lot of good advice and sensible comment as well as doctrinal information.

Professor Richard Gombrich, author of
What the Buddha Thought

This Being, That Becomes

The Buddha's Teaching on Conditionality

Dhivan Thomas Jones

Windhorse Publications

Published by
Windhorse Publications
169 Mill Road
Cambridge
CB1 3AN
UK

info@windhorsepublications.com
www.windhorsepublications.com

First edition 2011

Printed by Bell & Bain Ltd, Glasgow

Cover image and design by Stefanie Ine Grewe

British Library Cataloguing in Publication Data:
A catalogue record for this book is available from the British Library.

ISBN 9781 899579 90 7

Contents

Preface and Acknowledgements

This book is an introduction to the Buddha's core teaching of *paṭicca-samuppāda*, or dependent arising, which I refer to as 'conditionality', as well as an introduction to the application of this Buddhist wisdom in practice. To present Indian ideas of twenty-five centuries ago not as historical artefacts but as living spiritual teachings requires the translation of both letter and spirit into twenty-first-century conditions. As for the letter, I have gone back to the teaching of the Buddha as recorded in the Pali canon, and brought out as much as possible from that treasure house with the help of available scholarly resources. And as for the spirit, my approach relies on the teaching of Sangharakshita, founder of the Triratna Buddhist Community, whose presentation of the Buddha's teaching has always emphasized the centrality of dependent arising in Buddhist doctrine.

First and foremost among the conditions upon which this book has arisen has been Sagaraghosa. The initial idea for the book came from her, and the approach taken in it comes from her experience of teaching the Dharma at Cambridge Buddhist Centre. Our original intention was that we would co-author the book, but eventually I have written it while she has been collaborator, editor, critic, and support. However, she has contributed most of the questions at the end of each chapter, and her influence is everywhere in the practical examples and applications of abstract teachings.

I would like to thank Sagaramati and Jñanavaca for their perceptive comments on, and criticisms of, earlier drafts. Thanks also to Vidyadevi for her many astute questions and comments on a later draft. Kamalashila made some useful comments on the 24 *nidāna* reflection in the Appendix. Thanks to Caroline, Sarah, Priyananda and Amanda at Windhorse Publications, and to Saddharaja for drawing the spiral path diagram. I am grateful to Prof. Richard Gombrich and Dr Margaret Cone for what I have learned from them about Pali language and literature. Finally, I am more than grateful to Sangharakshita for founding the Triratna Buddhist Order and Community, the context and community in which these profound and practical ideas are embodied in a thriving contemporary tradition of Buddhist practice.

Dhivan Thomas Jones
Cambridge, October 2010

Publisher's acknowledgement

Windhorse Publications would like to express their thanks to the anonymous donor who made the publication of this book possible. We are very grateful.

List of Figures

Introduction

Buddhism and Conditionality

'Those things conditionally arisen ....'

Buddhism had almost died out in India, the land of its birth, by the thirteenth century CE, for reasons not well understood. Many of the old Buddhist sites disappeared beneath jungle and were forgotten. Then, in the nineteenth century, archaeologists enthusiastic about India's amazing history started locating and uncovering the ancient sacred places.[1] These discoveries played an important part in the gradual awakening of Europe and the west to the riches of the Buddhist religion. Among the ruins of ancient burial mounds and temples the archaeologists found thousands of little clay seals embossed with some verses in Sanskrit, the religious language of India both then and now:

> *ye dharmā hetuprabhavā hetuṃ teṣāṃ tathāgato hyavadat*
> *teṣāṃ ca yo nirodha evaṃ vādī mahāśramaṇaḥ*
>
> Those things conditionally arisen –
> the Realized One has told their cause,
> and the ceasing of them too;
> this is the great renouncer's teaching.[2]

Sometimes the clay seals were worn or broken; sometimes only the first few words of the verses – *ye dharmā hetuprabhavā* – had been cast. Different scripts were used, depending on where and when the seals were made. These same verses were found, and continue to be found, all over the Buddhist world – on seals, on miniature *stūpas* (burial mounds), and inscribed into carved images of Buddhas and bodhisattvas, attesting to their importance to followers of the Buddhist faith.

The verses are known in Sanskrit as the *pratītya-samutpāda-gāthā*, or 'verses on dependent arising'. *Pratītya-samutpāda*, or in Pali, *paṭicca-samuppāda*, translates as 'dependent arising' or 'dependent origination'.[3] This term refers to the teaching of conditionality – that things arise on conditions, and cease again when their conditions cease – and this teaching of conditionality is the fundamental principle taught by the Buddha. While the Sanskrit *pratītya-samutpāda-gāthā* are found on sculptures and seals dated to between the sixth and eleventh centuries CE, the verses themselves go back to the time of the historical Buddha, in the fifth century BCE.[4] The 'Realized One' or *tathāgata* is another title for the Buddha, as is 'great renouncer'. The verses say simply that the Buddha teaches the conditions under which things arise and cease again.

These verses are first recorded in the early scriptures as a teaching given by Assaji, one of the Buddha's first followers, to Sāriputta, who later became one of the Buddha's chief disciples. Sāriputta asked Assaji to give him the gist of the Buddha's Dharma, and Assaji responded with these verses. Just hearing them was enough for Sāriputta to experience a flash of insight into the nature of reality; enough for him and his friend Moggallāna to then seek out the Buddha, to become his full-time followers, and later to experience for themselves the full bliss of liberation.[5] (The full story of Sāriputta's conversion will be told in Chapter Two.)

This story suggests that for Sāriputta the verses taught by Assaji can be compared to the end of that golden thread imagined by the poet William Blake:

> I give you the end of a golden thread,
> Only wind it into a ball,
> It will let you in at Heaven's Gate
> Built in Jerusalem's Wall.[6]

In themselves the verses on dependent arising appear simple and straightforward. They point out a feature of reality that seems

Figure 1: *Bodhisattva Tārā, black basalt, 12th c., Bihar. The words 'ye dharmā hetuprabhavā . . . .' appear in the nimbus above Tārā's head, in the siddhaṃ script of eastern India.*

quite plain, namely that things arise due to various causes and conditions, and consequently cease when those same causes and conditions cease. However, it was the implications of this teaching of conditionality that Sāriputta intuited. The verses on dependent arising were the end of a golden thread that Sāriputta could wind in as he travelled the path of the Buddhas that leads to the ancient city of enlightenment.

The Buddhists of India therefore venerated those verses because they contain the essence of the Dharma, the Buddha's teaching. Scholars have often described the verses on dependent arising as a Buddhist 'creed', meaning an outline of the basic beliefs of the Buddhist religion. However, this description is misleading, as talk of a Buddhist 'creed' involves an inaccurate analogy with a very different religion. The verses do not represent a Buddhist 'creed'; rather, they point to a difficult truth that is to be fully understood, not merely believed in. For Buddhists this understanding or insight might begin from faith, but faith, in Buddhism, is a matter of trust rather than belief (this is more fully explored in Chapter Four). The verses on dependent arising express an understanding of reality that we might ourselves come to experience.

Despite the apparent simplicity of the teaching of conditionality, its implications – to which the golden thread leads – are deep and profound. The story goes that the Buddha, just after his enlightenment, considered that the Dharma was so difficult to understand and the truth of dependent arising so difficult to fathom that it would be a waste of time to try to teach it. Happily, the story continues, the god Brahmā intervened to convince the Buddha that some people would nevertheless be receptive to his teaching.[7] In another story the Buddha's companion, Ānanda, told the Buddha that although the teaching of dependent arising is deep and profound it seemed perfectly clear to him. The Buddha's resonant, solemn reply was this:

> Do not say that, Ānanda, do not say that. This dependent arising is deep and profound. It is from not understanding and penetrating this Dharma that people

> have become like a tangle of string covered in mould and matted like grass, unable to escape from samsara with its miseries, disasters, and bad destinies.[8]

Ānanda, it seems, underestimated the implications of dependent arising. It is because of not understanding and living from this truth that people are condemned to keep on suffering. These stories tell us that there is an important difference between a merely verbal and intellectual grasp of dependent arising and an emotional or existential insight into the liberating significance of the teaching in human experience. The verses on dependent arising are thus only the start of the journey, and the point is to follow the golden thread all the way.

As well as summarizing the essence of the Dharma, the verses on dependent arising may represent a way in which Indian Buddhists expressed their devotion to the Buddha.[9] After the great teacher died, one way in which his followers paid their respects to him was by honouring *stūpas* or burial mounds in which his cremated remains had been placed. But even in the Buddha's lifetime he equated himself not with his mere physical body but with the Dharma that he had realized and made known. A monk named Vakkali was once gravely ill, and asked the Buddha to visit him. When the Buddha did so, Vakkali expressed his remorse at not being well enough to have visited and paid his respects to the Buddha. But the Buddha put Vakkali's mind at ease:

> Enough, Vakkali, of your wanting to see my putrid body! Vakkali, who sees the Dharma sees me; who sees me sees the Dharma. Seeing the Dharma, Vakkali, you see me, and seeing me you see the Dharma.[10]

Vakkali needed only to honour and practise the Dharma in order to honour the Buddha.

The Buddha further equated the Dharma with his teaching of dependent arising when he said: 'Who sees *paṭicca-samuppāda* sees the Dharma; who sees the Dharma sees *paṭicca-samuppāda*.'[11] Therefore, the teaching of dependent arising is equated with the Buddha himself. The equations between the Buddha, the Dharma,

technical terms in Buddhism

bodhi

(the same in Pali and Sanskrit). This term is often translated 'enlightenment' but more accurately means 'awakening'. It is derived from the verbal root *budh*, which means 'understand' or 'awaken'. The word *buddha* also comes from this root, meaning 'one who has awakened', so the word *bodhi* refers to the state of a Buddha. Although the word 'enlightenment' is a common translation of *bodhi*, there was also a period in European history known as 'the Enlightenment', when science and rationality overtook religion in importance for understanding the world. However, the Buddha was not a scientist or rationalist, and his 'enlightenment' was more of an 'awakening' to the true nature of things from the sleep of spiritual ignorance.

and the teaching of conditionality became particularly important to Indian Buddhists of a later period. This is shown by the way the equations are made explicit in an early Mahāyāna text called the *Śālistamba Sūtra*:

> Monks, who sees *pratītya-samutpāda* sees the Dharma,
> and who sees the Dharma sees the Buddha.[12]

When they inscribed the verses on dependent arising onto sculptures, and cast them on thousands of little clay seals, the Indian Buddhists were therefore honouring the Buddha. When we study these verses, and the principle of conditionality that they express, we study not merely the beliefs of Buddhists but the very essence of the Dharma, and the true nature of the Buddha who taught it. To study them is to reach for the end of a golden thread stretching to enlightenment.

A presentation of conditionality

Several features of the Buddha's teaching of conditionality have already become apparent. Firstly, the teaching has been formulated in some simple verses that present it as a basic principle. Secondly, this basic principle has implications that lead to insight into the nature of reality. Thirdly, these implications are so profound that they are difficult to understand. For these reasons, although the Buddhist tradition as a whole has always remembered and honoured the basic principle of conditionality taught by the Buddha, the implications of it have been unfolded and explained in different ways according to need and circumstance.

My purpose in this book is to present the teaching of conditionality according to the way it was presented by the historical Buddha, but also in a pragmatic form useful for modern practitioners of the Buddhist path. Just because there have been so many interpretations of conditionality during the long history of Buddhism, I would like to go back to the source of these teachings, at least as far as it is possible to access them. This means investigating the Buddha's words as they are recorded in the Pali canon. This huge body of scriptures is the only one of several such collections of the Buddha's teachings to survive as a whole. It happens to be in the language now called Pali, which is derived from a North Indian dialect spoken in the Buddha's day, though that dialect was probably not the language that the Buddha himself spoke.

It is reasonable to wonder whether the discourses of the Pali scriptures were really spoken by the Buddha, or whether they were composed later. It is impossible to know for sure, because the teachings were passed on through an oral tradition for several centuries before they were written down. What is clear, however, is that the discourses and stories that have come down to us show a remarkable originality and consistency of thought, suggesting that the spiritual genius of a single individual, known as the Buddha, shines through them.[13] This book is designed to be a clear guide to the historical Buddha's teachings concerned with *paṭicca-samuppāda* as preserved in the Pali sources.

This presentation of conditionality is also an unfolding of the implications of the teaching in the circumstances of the modern world. Readers of this book may not be Buddhist monks or nuns, but you might consider yourself a dedicated practitioner of the Dharma. You might be familiar with ideas from science, psychology, and other spiritual traditions, though you might not have studied Buddhist philosophy. This book seeks to present the Buddha's teaching on conditionality in such a way that it is relevant and useful, contributing to an effective Dharma life.

In Part One, I present and explain the core teachings on *paṭicca-samuppāda* in the Pali scriptures. I follow the Buddha's example in using the teaching of conditionality to reflect on the human problem of *dukkha* or pain in its widest sense. While Chapters One and Two explore the principle of conditionality and the whole scope of its application, Chapter Three explores the chain of twelve links, or *nidānas*, that describe the origin of suffering and samsara, the endless cycle of rebirth.[14] Conditionality is also, however, the principle underlying the Buddha's teaching of the path that leads to the ending of suffering, and in Chapter Four I explain the factors of the path, arising in sequence, that lead to awakening.

In Part Two, I look more widely at applications and implications of conditionality. In Chapter Five I explore conditionality as applied to ethical behaviour, in the Buddha's teaching on karma. In Chapter Six I look at the idea of the Buddha's teaching as a 'middle way' in terms of lifestyle and philosophy. In Chapter Seven I go on to explore how conditionality implies universal impermanence (*aniccatā*) and lack of self (*anattā*), and in what sense nirvana is 'unconditioned'. Finally, in Chapter Eight, I turn my attention to how the later Buddhist tradition understood the Buddha's teaching on conditionality. I explore the important idea of *śūnyatā*, 'emptiness', and also that of 'mutual interpenetration', and I end with a consideration of how conditionality implies interdependence.

How to use this book

As well as being an introduction to early Buddhist teachings on conditionality, this book is designed as a reference work on *paṭicca-samuppāda* and as a practical guide to conditionality for individual or group study. Because of these several functions, a brief word on how to read the book might be useful.

The narrative structure means that the book is best read from beginning to end; I introduce concepts and ideas as I go along that will be assumed later on. Nevertheless, I have included a glossary of Pali and Sanskrit terms at the end, so that readers can look up Buddhist terms they come across without having to find where they were explained earlier in the text. I have also included text boxes that focus on particular 'technical terms in Buddhism' and draw attention to specific aspects of their meaning.

Readers will notice that this book contains a lot of numbered references to endnotes. These notes contain references to Pali discourses from which I quote, and to works I cite, and also add small discussions of certain points. All these are given for the benefit of those who would like to explore matters further. There is no need to refer to these notes at a first reading, and they can be safely ignored unless you would like more information.

You will also notice that at the end of each chapter I have included questions designed to create a link between general ideas and personal experience. I have in mind that you might pause at these points in your reading and engage with the text in a different way: you might pause for a period of personal reflection at the end of reading each chapter, using the questions to consider the implications of conditionality for your own life and practice; or you may skip the questions at a first reading, but return to them later or during a second perusal of the book. Or the questions may be used in the course of group study, to prompt reflection and discussion on how the teachings on conditionality might be applied.

Finally, I have included a guided '24 *nidāna* reflection' as an Appendix. This text is designed to guide a session of reflection and contemplation on the twelve *nidānas* of the 'Wheel of Life' together with the twelve *nidānas* of the 'spiral path', all of which are discussed in Part One of the book. It is based on a method for contemplating the 24 *nidānas* that was devised by Sangharakshita, and is used as a contemplative practice in the Triratna Buddhist Order. I hope that its inclusion may encourage you to spend time quietly contemplating the teaching of conditionality and allowing its implications to sink more fully into your awareness. An audio version of this guided reflection, lasting about 45 minutes, is available via www.freebuddhistaudio.com under 'meditation'.

Part One

Core Teachings on Conditionality

Chapter One

The Principle of Conditionality

The fundamental principle of the Dharma

The discourses of the Pali canon contain many stories about the Buddha and his encounters with various characters in the India of his day. In one of these stories, the Buddha fell into conversation with a religious wanderer named Sakuludāyin, who had previously been talking to a spiritual teacher who claimed to be omniscient; that is, he claimed to know everything through his extraordinary spiritual attainments. However, when Sakuludāyin asked this teacher some difficult questions about the past, he prevaricated and changed the subject, and Sakuludāyin was understandably disappointed. Knowing that the Buddha too had some spiritual attainment, Sakuludāyin asked him to comment on this topic of knowing the past. The Buddha's reply, however, was not what the wanderer had expected. Putting talk of omniscience aside, he said:

> But let the past be, Udāyi, let the future be. I will teach you the Dharma: this being, that becomes; from the arising of this, that arises. This not being, that does not become; from the ceasing of this, that ceases.[1]

That is, the Buddha simply drew Sakuludāyin's attention to how present experience arises according to the principle of conditionality. The moral of the story is that understanding conditionality is more important than comparing spiritual teachers.

The formula for conditionality that the Buddha taught to Sakuludāyin is the most common one found in the Pali scriptures:

> *imasmiṃ sati idaṃ hoti, imass'uppādā idaṃ uppajjati; imasmiṃ asati idaṃ na hoti, imassa nirodhā idaṃ nirujjhati.*
>
> This being, that becomes; from the arising of this, that arises.
> This not being, that does not become; from the ceasing of this, that ceases.[2]

This simple formula is honoured and chanted throughout the Buddhist world as the very essence of the Dharma. We can translate it into a contemporary idiom like this: *everything that exists has come into being dependent on particular causes and conditions; and when those causes and conditions cease, the things that depend on them will also cease.* With the rising of the sun, daylight arrives and the birds sing. With the death of a loved one, we experience grief. With your interest in the Dharma you have begun reading this book.

Despite the simplicity of this formula, some of the most profound and complex formulations of the Dharma are applications of the principle of conditionality that the formula expresses. The four noble truths, the twelve links (*nidānas*) of conditioned existence, and the factors of the 'spiral path' to liberation – all these teachings are applications of the principle of conditionality to the human situation. Conditionality might be compared to the simple musical scale upon which most western music is based. Just as the melodies of the Beatles and the operas of Mozart are based on this one musical scale, so different aspects of the Buddha's teaching are based on this one principle of conditionality. With this one principle the Buddha explained both why it is that human beings suffer, and how we can develop the wisdom to free ourselves from suffering.

A vision of human existence

However, our simple formula also contains within it a great mystery. Although the teaching of conditionality is at the heart of conceptual formulations of the Dharma, the Buddha also described the Dharma as 'beyond the sphere of reason' (*atakkāvacara*), meaning that it cannot ultimately be expressed in words or concepts: it has to be directly seen and known.[3] Hence conditionality is an entrance into a vision of reality, something at once more poetic and more powerful than a religious doctrine. The Buddha did not develop any one image that might help us imaginatively enter this vision, although he did mention the idea of a city bustling with life and activity to represent this dependently arisen world, as we will see below. The later Buddhist tradition developed the image of the Wheel of Life, which we will meet in Chapter Three, to represent the workings of conditioned existence, or samsara. In Chapter Four we will see that the Buddha also offered two images – one of waters flowing together into streams and rivers and flowing to the sea, and another of a tree coming into full leaf – as metaphors for the spiritual path unfolding in accordance with dependent arising. To find a poetic image that contains something of the Buddha's vision we might do worse than listen to William Blake:

> To see a World in a Grain of Sand,
> And a Heaven in a Wild Flower,
> Hold Infinity in the palm of your hand,
> And Eternity in an hour.[4]

To look at human experience from the perspective of conditionality is to encounter a vision of human existence that is at once challenging and exciting. This human body has arisen on certain conditions: the conditions of its conception, the conditions of its growth; even now it is sustained in existence by conditions such as food and air and by the continued reliable inner workings of our incredible organism; and it will inevitably cease when the conditions upon which it depends themselves cease. Our very sense of who we are, with our memories, dreams, and desires, arises on certain conditions – in this case not physical ones, but the intangible and delicate conditions of our background, ethnicity, nationality, and education; also, according to Buddhist teaching, our past actions (or karma) cast their shadow over, or lend their light to, present experience. We live at the quivering centre of a web of conditions so complex that while we can believe that it is all dependently arisen, exactly how or why any particular thought or feeling arises is mostly beyond our capacity to understand. Our bodies affect our moods; our feelings affect our thoughts; we all affect one another, for better or worse; our individual worlds are so interconnected that we may discover our truest selves only in solitude. In the midst of all this interdependence we find ourselves faced with the disorienting perception that there is nothing to hold onto that will not some day change and pass away.

The question now arises of where we can find lasting satisfaction and happiness in this obviously unreliable situation. No doubt there is a fantastic thrill in riding the glittering surf of our good fortune, while it lasts, or in abandoning ourselves to the intoxication of the cosmic dance. Life can sometimes seem amazing. But things go wrong because nothing lasts, and in any case life is not in our control. However, the Buddha's teaching points to a different kind of happiness and satisfaction that comes from a calm insight into the workings of things. The Buddha was born into this interdependent, impermanent world of experience just as we have been born. The task he set himself, however, was to discover whether there is some escape from the intrinsic unsatisfactoriness or *dukkha* of constant change. His search for that which is not subject to birth, old age and death took him through both meditative bliss (which did not last outside meditation) and painful austerity (which produced no liberation). Finally he came to see directly the law of conditionality by which the universe operates. Directly seeing it, he was able to see exactly how to live in a way which no longer gives rise to *dukkha*.

The Dharma as a practical teaching

This concern with *dukkha* marks the practical emphasis of the Dharma. Although the Buddha no doubt spent quite a bit of his time seeing the world in a grain of sand, he was quite down to earth about the scope of his teaching, saying: 'I teach only *dukkha* and the ending of *dukkha*'.[5] The Pali word *dukkha* means 'pain' or 'suffering', but also has the much wider connotation of 'unsatisfactoriness' and 'discontent'. The Buddha's emphasis on *dukkha* is not a sign of pessimism so much as a reminder that Buddhism starts from ordinary human experience. The first of the Buddha's four noble truths (which we will explore more fully in Chapter Two) is simply that 'there is *dukkha*'. The Dharma is fundamentally a practical teaching about how to find release from suffering and unhappiness, or, to put it positively, to attain enlightenment or awakening; and the Buddha used the framework of conditionality mainly to describe the arising and the passing away of this *dukkha*.

Let us put this practical emphasis into a bigger context. To study conditionality is really to study everything, since the principle of conditionality is that *everything that exists has come into being dependent on particular causes and conditions; and when those causes and conditions cease, the things that depend on them will also cease*. Indeed, when put like this, the principle sounds quite familiar; the whole tradition of western scientific thought is based on a similar assumption – that the universe is a cosmos, an ordered whole, everything in it arising on causes and conditions. Both Buddhism and western science believe that the universe has come about through natural laws and processes. However, whereas western science has been primarily interested in investigating the laws that govern the working of the external world, Buddhism has mostly been interested in the mind – the inner world of consciousness – and not just theoretically but in practical ways that help human beings find inner liberation.

In fact, the historical Buddha seems not to have been interested in trying to explain the mysteries of the universe, or even the world around him. His attention was on the practical business

technical terms in Buddhism

dukkha

(in Pali; in Sanskrit *duḥkha*). This term is hard to translate in one English word. It is used as an adjective to describe feelings that are 'unpleasant' and 'painful', but it is also used as an abstract noun to describe a primary characteristic of conditioned existence. It can be translated as 'suffering' – but sometimes conditioned existence is not that bad. It can be translated as 'unsatisfactoriness', but this is a bit weak. It can be translated just as 'unhappiness', 'unease', or 'discontentment' in the broadest sense. Some scholars trace it back to *duḥ* (a prefix meaning 'bad' or 'difficult') + *kha* (meaning the 'axle' of a cart). So an image for *dukkha* is that life is a rough and bumpy ride. A solution often followed in this book is to leave the word untranslated.

of inner development, and even his observations of the natural world were mainly metaphors for explaining the workings of the mind.[6] The practical spiritual emphasis of conditionality seems to have been radical even in the Buddha's own time. The term *paṭicca-samuppāda*, which I render 'conditionality', means 'dependent arising' or 'dependent origination'. The expression is just as awkward in the original Indian language as in English, and it was probably invented by the Buddha to give expression to his awakened insight.[7] It indicates a new way of looking at things, one that was not interested in speculating about what things ultimately exist or do not exist, but was concerned with what is important for understanding human experience.

The Buddha's teaching did not spring only from his awakened mind; it also had an intellectual and historical context. Knowing a little about this context helps us to understand better why the Buddha expressed himself in certain ways. For instance, among the many metaphysical theories about ultimate reality in circulation in the Buddha's day was an opposed pair with which the Buddha often contrasted his own teaching. According to the first theory, common among the brahman sages who studied the Upaniṣads, there is an eternal, unchanging ground of being (*Brahman*) which is the ultimate reality of things, and the point of the spiritual life is to gain access through meditation to the unchanging inner self (the *ātman*), and hence become one with reality. According to the opposing theory, held by certain wandering philosophers, the world is a product of chance combinations of elements, and in this way of explaining things, there is no point to life except what you make of it. The Buddha's teaching of dependent arising offered a point of view quite different to these two (which he called a 'middle way', and which we will study in Chapter Six). If everything arises on conditions, then through understanding these conditions it becomes possible to cultivate wholesome conditions and remove unhelpful ones. This is a much more practical view of the spiritual life than one based on a metaphysical theory.

In the Pali scriptures there is a story that vividly illustrates the Buddha's point of view in contrast to ideas of his day. A monk called Māluṅkyaputta approached the Buddha and threatened to disrobe and leave the monastic order unless the Buddha told him the answers to some difficult metaphysical questions:

1. whether the universe is eternal, or
2. whether the universe is not eternal;
3. whether the universe is finite, or
4. whether the universe is infinite;
5. whether the soul and the body are the same, or
6. whether the soul and the body are different; and
7. whether a *tathāgata* (a Buddha) exists after death, or
8. whether a *tathāgata* does not exist after death, or
9. whether a *tathāgata* both exists and does not exist after death, or
10. whether a tathāgata neither exists nor does not exist after death.

This list of ten questions occurs frequently in the Pali scriptures as a standard set of metaphysical questions that the Buddha refuses to answer. The questions represent some standard 'big issues' that wandering religious teachers like the Buddha were supposed to have opinions on. We could probably think of contemporary equivalents: is there intelligent life elsewhere in the universe, or not? Can consciousness be explained in material terms alone, or not? And so on.

The Buddha refused to answer, telling Māluṅkyaputta that he was like a man who has been shot in the eye with an arrow smeared with poison, but who will not allow the doctor to remove the arrow (representing *dukkha*) unless he is first told who shot the arrow, their name and family, the colour of their hair, and so on. The Buddha went on to tell Māluṅkyaputta that he left the answers to those metaphysical questions 'undeclared' (*avyākata*) because they are irrelevant:

> They are not connected with the goal, they are not fundamental to the spiritual life (*brahmacariya*), they do not conduce to disenchantment, to dispassion, to cessation, to peacefulness, to wisdom, to awakening, or to nirvana.[8]

Even if we could answer our own fascinating metaphysical questions we would be no nearer to awakening. What he does teach, the Buddha told Māluṅkyaputta, is the nature of *dukkha*, how it arises and ceases, and the path to its cessation, which is the same thing as the path to awakening and nirvana. That is to say, the Buddha told Māluṅkyaputta that what he taught was the application of conditionality to the problem of human unhappiness. And that is all.

An example – stress

Let us pause in our exploration of the general principle of conditionality to consider what it means in relation to an example of *dukkha*. I will consider a form of *dukkha* with which most of us will be familiar – the experience of stress. By 'stress' I mean the painful mental and emotional tension that arises when we are under demanding or adverse circumstances, the kind of stress that involves symptoms such as physical pain, muscular tensions, poor sleep and headaches. First, let us consider those conditions on which such experience of stress arises. The diagram below shows a few of them:

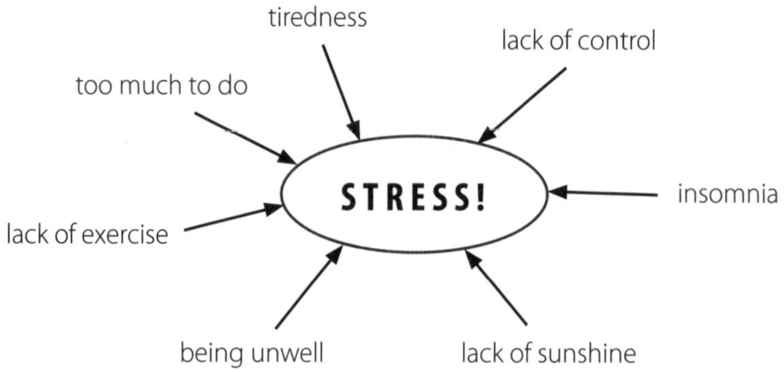

If we were to use the general formula of conditionality to express how stress arises, we would say: *when there is too much to do, when there is tiredness, lack of control, and so on, then there is stress. From the arising of these factors, stress arises.* The Buddha's general principle of conditionality is a form of words that allows us to describe our experience in a way that avoids unnecessary mystification or personal blame. We may not know exactly why we have become stressed, but we can identify some factors that are most probably responsible.

On further reflection, however, the reality of stress is more complicated than this simple diagram allows. Most of these factors that cause stress are themselves affected when one is stressed. If you feel tired, that might contribute to your feeling stressed, but the stress itself might then cause you to feel more tired. Feeling unwell might stress you a bit, but then the stress itself might make you feel even more unwell. Our experience is not something that, once it arises, stays the same until some conditions change, but it is something in constant change, with different factors influencing one another in a complex process. We can represent this in a second diagram:

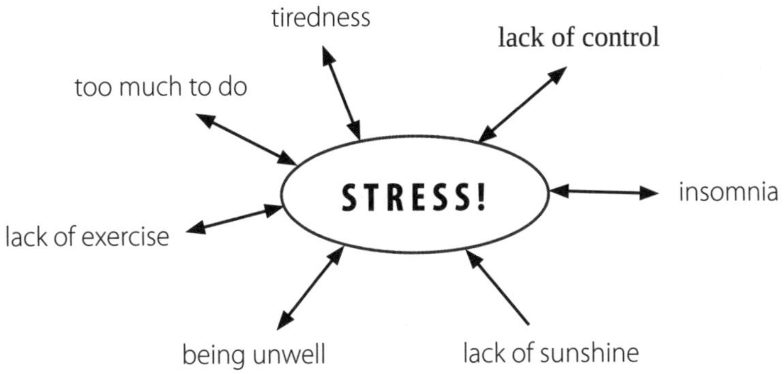

But we might now go on to notice that we cannot isolate stress in our experience, thinking it is the only thing that arises on conditions. Some of the factors that give rise to stress are also involved in the arising of other factors that give rise to stress, in a play of mutual influence. For instance, if you are unwell, you are less likely to take exercise, and lack of exercise might cause you to be more unwell. Not every factor affects everything else, of course; the web of conditions is very complex. Another diagram shows how it is beginning to look:

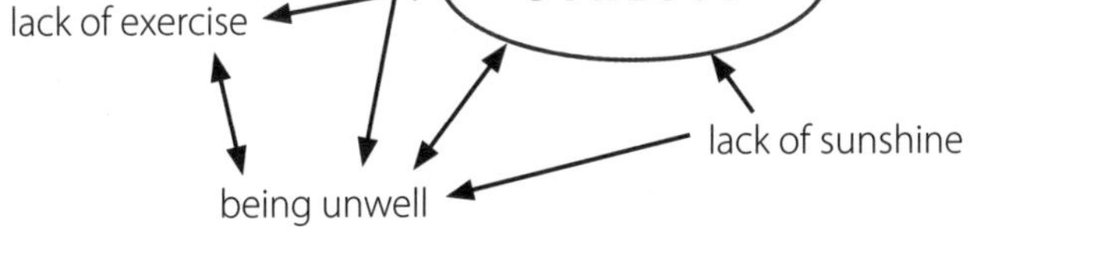

Even such an apparently isolated aspect of our experience as stress turns out to exist in a complex interdependent web of conditions and dependent arising. This very complexity no doubt partly explains why we become stressed – because it is not easy for us to understand how all the conditions operate whereby our particular bodies and minds begin to experience stress.

So stress arises. Stress is *dukkha,* painful and unsatisfactory. How can we make it stop? If we continue to explore the Buddha's teaching of conditionality, we might consider how stress ceases when the conditions on which it arose cease. If we are to enjoy some relief from stress, and to find a sense of relaxation and openness in life again, then it is necessary for us to identify and remove those conditions that are the most significant for the arising of stress. Once we take action to remove those conditions – lessen our workload, have some sleep, take some exercise – the stress that arose on conditions of these factors will cease. *When there is not too much to do, when you aren't so tired, when you feel a little more in control, then there's less stress. From the ceasing of these factors, stress ceases.* And while the dynamic tangle of conditions on which stress arises is complex, the good news is that we might only have to change one crucial factor to affect all the rest. Just taking a little more exercise, for instance, might help you sleep better, so you feel less tired, you feel more able to do what needs to be done, and your stress dips back down beneath the threshold of discomfort so that you find yourself moving back into a more effective and enjoyable experience.

This simple consideration of the conditions under which stress arises is an example of paying wise attention (*yoniso manasikāra*) to our experience. Through paying wise attention we find ourselves in a better position to make good decisions about changes we can make in our lives. Paying attention is, in fact, one of the most powerful positive conditions for change; in Chapter Four we will see that the Buddha taught that wise attention is one of the conditions for the arising of the Buddhist path. In present-day psychology, the practice of awareness of the body and of thoughts is recognized as one of the most effective means of alleviating the *dukkha* of stress.[9] Awareness enables us to make choices instead of living on 'automatic pilot'. With awareness as condition, we can do small things that help us overcome a feeling of being out of control, such as developing a different relationship to thoughts; for instance, to the thought *there's too much to do.*

The difference between 'causes' and 'conditions'

Considering stress as an example of *dukkha* has enabled us to see how a particular experience arises on various conditions, and changes or ceases when those conditions change or cease. Let us now compare conditions with causes, for the sake of better understanding exactly what is meant by conditionality. In ordinary language, the *cause* of some event is what is immediately responsible for its occurrence, whereas a *condition* is any supporting factor. We did not find a single *cause* for stress so much as a set of *conditions* under which stress arose. To take another example, we might say that the *cause* of someone's death might be said to be a heart attack or cancer, but there are very many more *conditions* that may have played a part in this death, such as diet, habits, and lifestyle. Conditionality is therefore a broader concept than causality. There is no one cause of *dukkha*, but many conditions for its arising.

This is implied by the Buddha's general formula. The statement 'this being, that becomes' suggests the most general quality of one thing being the condition for another. An example given by the Buddha is the relation of birth to ageing and death (the eleventh and twelfth of the twelve *nidānas*, which we will study in Chapter Five). The Buddha is reported to have reflected on this relation as follows:

> Monks, before my awakening, when I was still an unawakened bodhisatta, I had this thought: 'How this world is fallen! It is born, it ages, it dies, it passes away and it re-arises. And no one knows how to escape from *dukkha*, from ageing and death. When will an escape from *dukkha*, from ageing and death, be discovered?'
>
> Then, monks, I had this thought: 'When what exists does ageing and death exist? From what as condition is there ageing and death?' From paying wise attention I came to realize through insight that: 'When there is birth then ageing and death exist; with birth as condition, there is ageing and death.'[10]

We see in this example that 'birth' and 'ageing and death' replace the 'this' and 'that' of the general formula. We would not say that birth was the *cause* of ageing and death (there might be an immediate cause, such as cancer or other illness, and more general causes, such as lifestyle), but only that birth is the *condition* for ageing and death: without birth, there could be no ageing and death.[11]

The distinction of causes from conditions becomes important when we consider the second of the Buddha's four noble truths (see Chapter Two), namely that 'the origin of *dukkha* is craving'. This important teaching is often translated 'the cause of suffering is craving or desire'. However, the Buddha's teaching is not that craving is the *cause* of *dukkha;* instead it is the most important among the many conditions upon which *dukkha* arises for a conscious human being.

In Chapter Three we will discover how the twelve *nidānas* of *paṭicca-samuppāda*, the Buddha's usual way of teaching conditionality, can be understood as describing twelve connected conditions for the arising of *dukkha* in human experience. Craving is one of the twelve *nidānas*, but craving itself arises dependent on several conditions. Our stress and our suffering therefore arise not through one cause, but through many connected conditions, each playing their part in supporting the wrong views and unwholesome behaviour that lead to different kinds of pain. Consequently, the way that leads from *dukkha* to insight and awakening consists in changing these conditions, each changed condition influencing the rest. Needless to say, the human situation is complicated, and each of us is uniquely complicated. Nevertheless, conditionality is the basic principle that allows us all to work out a path to well being.

Conditionality as a transcendental principle

The various doctrines and methods of the Dharma are ways in which we can usefully apply the principle of conditionality to the human situation. However, the pragmatic focus of Buddhism is effective because the principle of conditionality is objective and universal. The word 'Dharma' is related to a Sanskrit verbal root *dhṛ*, meaning 'to bear' or 'to hold up', and it means both 'teaching' and 'reality'. The Dharma in the sense of the Buddha's teaching is the foundation for living in accordance with the Dharma in the sense of the nature of reality. This Dharma, being ultimately beyond words and concepts, is fully known only by being directly seen. Conditionality, the Buddha's teaching of *paṭicca-samuppāda*, is the principal doctrine by which the Buddha managed to express something of his direct realization of the Dharma. Therefore the Buddha taught conditionality as the fundamental conceptual expression of the Dharma:

> One who sees dependent arising (*paṭicca-samuppāda*) sees the Dharma; one who sees the Dharma sees dependent arising.[12]

Conditionality is therefore a 'transcendental principle' of the Dharma, meaning an expression in words of the nature of reality that ultimately transcends words and concepts.[13]

As well as being 'transcendental' in the sense of expressing a reality beyond words, the principle of conditionality is 'transcendental' in the sense that it applies to all experience whatever; it is an objective and universal feature of experience. One way in which the Buddha expressed this was by saying that things arise on conditions whether or not anyone notices, and whether or not there are Buddhas who have awoken to it:

> What, monks, is dependent arising? With birth as condition, monks, there is age and death. Whether or not *tathāgatas* [i.e. Buddhas] arise, this natural condition persists, this stability of reality, this fixed course of things, just this conditionality.[14]

The Buddha repeats this teaching for the relationship of each of the twelve *nidānas*, reinforcing the universal scope of *paṭicca-samuppāda*. The point is that the Dharma is not *just* the Buddha's good idea, and not *only* a useful teaching; it is based on the nature of reality, whether or not any awakened beings have realized it.

The Buddha also expressed the objectivity and universality

of his teaching in terms of a beautiful simile, that of the path to awakening as an old road, and awakening itself as an ancient city, known by former Buddhas, and rediscovered, restored and renewed by him:

> Monks, it is as if a man walking about in a wooded wilderness should see an old path, an unwinding old road travelled by people of former times: that man would follow it, and following it would see an old city, an ancient capital city inhabited by people of former times, a city having lovely parks, groves, and ponds, and with a raised mound around it.
>
> Then, monks, that man would tell his king or the prime minister about it, saying, 'Your Majesty should know that, while walking about in a wooded wilderness, I saw an old path, an unwinding old road travelled by people of former times; I followed it and, following it, I saw an old city, an ancient capital city inhabited by people of former times, a city having lovely parks, groves, and ponds, and with a raised mound around it. Sir, please restore it!' Then, monks, the king or prime minister would restore that city, and after some time it might become prosperous and powerful, rich and populous, as successful as it had been before.
>
> In the same way, monks, I saw an old path, an unwinding old road travelled by Buddhas of former times. And what, monks, is this old path, this unwinding old road travelled by Buddhas of former times? It is just this noble eightfold path, namely, right view . . . [and so on, up to right concentration]. This, monks, is the old path, the unwinding old road travelled by Buddhas of former times. I followed it and, following it, understood ageing and death; I understood the arising of ageing and death; I understood the cessation of ageing and death; and I understood the path leading to the cessation of ageing and death . . . .[15]

> Having understood all this, I have told the monks, nuns and lay-followers about it. This spiritual life (*brahmacariya*), monks, has become prosperous and powerful, well known and popular, widespread and well declared among gods and human beings.[16]

Each of us, in following the path of the Dharma, is in a sense rediscovering the ancient road to awakening that the Buddha found after it had become lost. This road, like the principle of conditionality, has always been there ready to be discovered.

The difficulty of the Dharma

However, even if we find the Dharma and begin to walk the ancient road of the Buddhas, made of the transcendental principle which is conditionality, we will not necessarily find the Dharma easy to practise. Although the principle of conditionality is easy to state and sounds somewhat obvious, its consequences in practice are profound, and understanding them is by no means straightforward. After all, if it were easy to see the way conditionality works, we would already have noticed what it is that causes us difficulty in life, and changed

technical terms in Buddhism

nirvāṇa

(in Sanskrit; in Pali *nibbāna*) is, like *dukkha*, almost untranslatable. Literally it means a 'going out' and the word is used with reference to extinguishing a flame. Metaphorically the word refers to the 'going out' of the passions and of ignorance – the quenching of the burning fires of greed, hate, and delusion. *Nirvāṇa* does not mean the extinguishing of the person or the personality, only of the root causes of *dukkha*. But the way *nirvāṇa* is used in the Buddhist scriptures also shows it has positive connotations – of complete happiness and satisfaction. It is the word used in early Indian religious and spiritual thought to mean the *summum bonum*, the highest good in life, and the ultimate goal of spiritual striving.

it. We would have fixed the wonky axle on our carts and would be living happily. But our experience is often enough like a tangled ball of string – we sort out one thing, but life knots up somewhere else.

The situation is summed up in another story from the Pali canon, this one from the Ariyapariyesanā Sutta, or 'Discourse on the Noble Quest', an important early discourse in which the Buddha recounts some of his earlier life. It is said that after the Buddha gained awakening, he spent time just sitting beneath the Goatherds' Banyan Tree on the bank of the river Nerañjarā, near the village of Uruvelā (modern day Bodhgaya in Bihar). The Goatherds' Banyan was probably some magnificent ancient tree, a mass of columns and shady leaves, under which the local goatherds liked to shelter from the sun. It is said that the Buddha spent some days there, simply enjoying and reflecting on the bliss of awakening. While doing so he contemplated how he could teach others the way to the breakthrough he had achieved. But:

> While the Blessed One was secluded and alone, the following thought occurred to him: 'The Dharma that I have discovered is profound, difficult, abstruse, serene, rarefied, non-conceptual, subtle, only to be known by the wise. But this world is ensconced in pleasure, enjoyment, and delight; and, the world being so ensconced, it is difficult for people to fathom the perspective of conditionality and dependent arising, and hard too for them to make sense of nirvana, that final dispassionate perspective in which all formations are calm, all that is borne is given up, and craving is extinguished. If I were to teach the Dharma, and others did not understand me, it would be a wearisome bother for me.'[17]

The story goes that at this point the god Brahmā arrived and persuaded the Buddha that there were beings who would be able to understand. The Buddha then had a vision of human beings as like lotuses – some living under water, some just emerged, and some fully flowering out of the water, unsmeared by it. In the same way there were some people who would be able to understand the Dharma. And so the Buddha decided to teach.

This story reminds us of the Buddha's words to Ānanda, who had exclaimed that dependent arising seemed perfectly clear to him. 'Do not say that, Ānanda,' the Buddha replied:

> This dependent arising is deep and profound. It is from not understanding and penetrating this Dharma that people have become like a tangle of string covered in mould and matted like grass, unable to escape from samsara with its miseries, disasters, and bad destinies.[18]

This suggests that although the principle of conditionality is relatively easy to understand, such an understanding may not get to the heart of what the Buddha meant. On the one hand, the Dharma is difficult because the reality of things lies beyond words and concepts, and the principle of conditionality is an expression of this ineffable truth. On the other hand, the Dharma is difficult because people are 'ensconced in pleasure, enjoyment, and delight'. We are emotionally bound up with the content of our experience so that we remain unaware of how it all arises on conditions. To study and understand conditionality, then, is to begin to untangle the knots in our emotions and views that bind us into human suffering.

Questions for Chapter One

1. Draw a diagram to show which conditions lead you to feel more stressed and the relationships between them. Which of those conditions can you most easily change?
2. Reflect on some positive change you have made in your life. It might be something quite mundane, such as learning to drive a car, or some change in behaviour such as starting to meditate regularly. Draw a diagram to show the conditions that contributed to that positive change. Draw arrows to show the relationships between those conditions.
3. Reflect on some positive change you would like to make, and the conditions that would contribute to making that change. Draw a diagram to show the relationship between these conditions. Which of the conditions is it easiest for you to bring into being or cultivate more?

Chapter Two

The Scope of Conditionality

In Chapter One I introduced *paṭicca-samuppāda*, or conditionality, as the fundamental principle of the Buddha's teaching. We dwelt on the very idea of conditionality, of everything in existence arising on certain conditions and ceasing when those conditions cease. We saw that this conception was a formula sufficient for the Buddha to explain everything that it is necessary to know for his followers to understand the arising and ceasing of *dukkha*. In this chapter I consider how the principle is applied in the four noble truths, a teaching that summarizes the whole scope of conditionality, from the arising of conditioned existence to its ceasing in nirvana.

The conversions of Sāriputta and Moggallāna

But first another story. There were once two spiritual seekers for whom hearing the Buddha's teaching of conditionality initiated a conversion process culminating in their becoming *arahants*, or awakened beings. In the India of the Buddha's day, there was a well-established tradition of spiritual seekers leaving home to become *samaṇas* who sought the truth in meditation, asceticism, and philosophical debate. The *samaṇas* (in Sanskrit, *śramaṇas*) were literally 'strivers', living on alms, wearing cast-off clothes and wandering without a home (though women needed the protection of a *saṅgha*, or community). The Buddha himself had gone forth from family life to become such a seeker; and even after his own awakening he continued to live on alms, as a wandering *samaṇa*.

Sāriputta and Moggallāna (whose names may be more familiar in their Sanskrit forms, Śāriputra and Maudgalyāyana) were friends who, like the Buddha, had embarked upon a spiritual quest, leaving home to join the *samaṇas*. They first practised under a teacher called Sañjaya, who was probably more of a philosopher than an ascetic.[1] However, they had a mutual agreement that whoever first discovered the 'Deathless' would tell the other about it. The Deathless is not physical immortality, since awakened beings die just like everyone else; rather, it refers to a state in which one has transcended birth, death, and suffering – a state synonymous with nirvana.[2] Sāriputta and Moggallāna wished to find out about this ultimate realization. Then, so the story goes, Sāriputta came across Assaji (in Sanskrit, Aśvajit), one of the Buddha's first disciples:

> One morning the Venerable Assaji, having dressed and taken his robe and bowl, went into Rājagaha for alms. He entered and left houses, he looked in front and behind, he bent and straightened his limbs, all with composure, his eyes cast down and his movements graceful. Sāriputta the wanderer saw the Venerable Assaji on his almsround so composed as he entered and left houses, as he looked in front and behind, as he bent and straightened his limbs, his eyes cast down and his movements graceful, and seeing him he thought to himself, 'if anyone in the world is an *arahant* or has attained the path to *arahant*-ship, this monk is one of them. What if I were to approach him and ask: "Friend, under whom have you gone forth, who is your teacher, whose Dharma do you profess?"' But then Sāriputta the wanderer thought to himself, 'Now is not the time to question this monk – he is on his almsround among the houses. But what if I were to follow close behind him, in pursuit of what he knows?'
>
> When the Venerable Assaji had finished his almsround in Rājagaha, he took his almsfood and left the city. Then Sāriputta the wanderer approached Venerable Assaji and

greeted him. When they had exchanged courteous and friendly greetings, Sāriputta the wanderer stood to one side and said to Venerable Assaji:

'Friend, your aura is shining and your complexion is pure and bright. Under whom have you gone forth, who is your teacher, whose Dharma do you profess?'

'Friend,' replied Venerable Assaji, 'there is a son of the Sakyas who has gone forth from the Sakya people, a great renunciate (*samaṇa*) – I have gone forth under that Blessed One, that Blessed One is my teacher, and I profess the Dharma of that Blessed One.'

'But what is the teaching of the Venerable's teacher; what does he declare?'

'Friend, I am a beginner, recently gone forth, not long come to this Dharma and discipline. I am not able to teach you the Dharma fully, though I can tell you its meaning in brief.'

Then Sāriputta the wanderer said this to Venerable Assaji:

'Friend, speak as much or as little as you like, but tell me the meaning at once. What matters to me is just the spirit; why spell out the letter?'

Then Venerable Assaji told Sāriputta the wanderer this formulation of the Dharma:

> Those things conditionally arisen –
> the Realized One has told their cause,
> and the ceasing of them too;
> this is the great renouncer's teaching.[3]

Hearing this formulation of the Dharma, the spotless, stainless vision of Dharma arose in Sāriputta the wanderer, that whatever is of a nature to arise will naturally cease, and he said:

> 'If this is indeed the truth (*dhamma*), then you have attained the state free from grief, unseen and neglected by so many for myriads of aeons.'[4]

Having encountered Assaji and having had a first insight into the Buddha's liberating teaching, Sāriputta at once set off to find Moggallāna, who saw him coming in the distance and noticed his friend's excitement. Moggallāna asked, 'Have you perhaps discovered the Deathless?' To which Sāriputta replied, 'Yes, friend, it is found.' He told Moggallāna the story of his meeting with Assaji, and the two friends soon departed to meet the Buddha, under whom they became monks. Later they became *arahants* and were regarded as two foremost disciples of the Buddha.

What was it about Venerable Assaji's words that made such an impression on Sāriputta? There would seem to be something missing. Perhaps in reality Assaji said a little more than that two-line summary of the Dharma. Or perhaps Sāriputta saw in Venerable Assaji's appearance, in his deportment and his composure, the signs of someone who had found the Deathless that he himself was looking for. He didn't need to be persuaded that Assaji was awakened – he wanted to know the teaching that had led to his awakening. When Assaji told him that things (*dhammas*) arise on certain conditions and cease when those conditions cease, the profound implications unwound at once. The liberating truth of the Deathless was not a matter for philosophical speculation, nor something realized through austerities; it was to be understood in the moment, in the way that things came about and passed away again. Venerable Assaji's exemplary awareness was a clue to how this teaching was to be put into practice. Sāriputta's eyes were opened, and he was on the path.

Sāriputta and Moggallāna therefore became converts to the Buddha's teaching when they caught a glimpse of what the path to the Deathless implies. Such faith based on personal experience is a condition for the unfolding of the Buddhist path to liberation. The spiritual life does not depend on holding the right beliefs (as some religions claim) or convincing oneself that one has grasped the truth intellectually (as some philosophers might think). Nor does it mean trying by force to free the mind from its unhappiness (as ascetics believe). Instead, the path to the Deathless starts when we gain a first-hand, clear-sighted awareness of how human experience works.

Reactive mind and creative mind

This clear-sighted awareness is therefore the pivotal factor in the spiritual quest, marking the beginning of a revolution or conversion in experience, such as that undergone by Sāriputta and Moggallāna. It must be said that awareness by no means sorts out all of our *dukkha*. In fact it can seem to make it more intense, since if we become more aware we usually experience ourselves more fully. Sangharakshita has characterized the revolution initiated by awareness in terms of a shift from a 'reactive' mode of mental functioning to a 'creative' mode:[5]

> The distinction which these modes represent is of fundamental importance not only in the 'system' of Buddhism but also in the spiritual life generally and even in the entire scheme of human evolution. The transition from 'reactive' to 'creative' marks, indeed, the beginning of spiritual life. It is conversion in the true sense of the term. What, then, do we mean by speaking of 'reactive mind' and 'creative mind'?[6]

When we talk of someone being 'reactive', we usually mean that they are particularly prickly or defensive, or that they tend towards passivity in their lives rather than being proactive. Sangharakshita, however, uses the term 'reactive mind' in a much more general sense to characterize the sense-based mentality that reacts to stimuli, a conditioned identification with upbringing, culture, education, and surroundings, which is unaware of all this except in a superficial way. Such a mind is metaphorically asleep.

Most people, most of the time, live through the reactive mind, as it is one of humankind's basic existential strategies.[7] Thrown into existence by forces unknown to us, we develop a sense of identity and belonging as best we can. Faced with difficulty as we go about our lives, our response is often unthinking and automatic, relying on instincts and emotions that are innate or inherited. Each time we respond to life in this way, the tendency is reinforced, further embedding us in a habitual life lived through habits to which we have long grown accustomed. The result is like revolving on a wheel, and indeed the Wheel of Life is a traditional Buddhist representation of samsara:

> It is clear that the Wheel of Life is able to symbolize the workings of the reactive mind because the reactive mind is itself a wheel. Like a wheel, it simply goes round and round. Prompted by negative emotions springing from the depths of unawareness, it again and again reacts to stimuli impinging on it from the outside world, and again and again precipitates itself into one or another sphere or mode of conditioned existence. Moreover, the wheel is a machine, perhaps the most primitive of all machines, and as such the Wheel of Life represents the mechanical and repetitive nature of the reactive mind.[8]

We will meet the Wheel of Life directly in Chapter Three. Meanwhile, these evocations of the reactive mind should not be taken as a judgement. The reactive mind is not bad or wrong; it is just a characterization of the unawakened human state. You could pause now as you read, and cast your mind back over the previous hour of your day. How many actions and decisions did you make without much conscious awareness? Looking back now, can you recall familiar patterns of thought that replayed themselves in your mind? If you had a conversation with someone, did your words and thoughts rehearse old points of view? The repetitious nature of much of our experience reveals the familiar presence of the reactive mind.

The fundamental characteristic of the reactive mind is its lack of awareness. It is the mind that is not aware of what it is doing. When our minds are functioning in the reactive mode we are not particularly aware of the conditions upon which our experience is arising, relying instead on our capacity to respond automatically.

Some of us will be familiar with an extreme example of this mode of functioning: after driving for a time on a familiar route we realize we have no recollection whatever of the previous few minutes or miles, despite having steered, braked, changed gears, and negotiated junctions. But we might be on 'automatic pilot' in less dramatic ways all through the day: as we walk; as we eat; as we wash, or clean our teeth; as we travel to work. Only when something breaks our routine, like illness or snowy weather, does our experience regain any freshness. And even then we might soon readjust or slip back into familiar ways. Looking at all this from the perspective of conditionality, we could say that the reactive mind makes it possible for patterns of negative emotion and fixed views to continue unquestioned. We remain entangled in conditions that give rise to *dukkha* and do nothing to discover or change them. When we are in this state, 'conditionality' might as well just be a word in a book about Buddhism.

By contrast, the 'creative mind' refers here not to the artistic impulse but to a mind that responds in a conscious and deliberate way to its experience. Through a long practice of awareness such a mind has become free of automatic responses, and is clear, open, and spontaneous. In personal relationships this amounts to an openness that is capable of receiving another person as they are. Faced with a difficult situation in life, someone who is functioning through the creative mind is not swept away by automatic reactions, but through awareness maintains a freedom of thought and feeling that allows a wise and kind response:

> The creative mind is above all the aware mind. Being aware ... the creative mind is also intensely and radiantly alive. The creative person, as one in whom the creative mind manifests may be termed, is not only more aware than the reactive person but possessed of far greater vitality. This vitality is not just animal high spirits or emotional exuberance, much less still mere intellectual energy or the compulsive urgency of egoistic volition. Were such expressions permissible, one might say it is the Spirit of Life itself rising like a fountain from

the infinite depths of existence, and vivifying, through the creative person, all with whom it comes into contact.[9]

Sangharakshita's poetic evocation of the 'Spirit of Life' here reminds us that the creative mind is just as much a natural human state as the reactive mind. Our capacity for conscious awareness is part of what makes us human, and the creative mind is the full exercising of that awareness. When we function through the creative mind we are simply more fully alive.

The four noble truths

When our minds are functioning in the reactive mode, we continue to create conditions for *dukkha* to arise. But when, through the arising of awareness, we begin to operate in the creative mode, we no longer create so many conditions for *dukkha* to arise, and we have embarked on the path that leads to nirvana and the end of suffering. All this was expressed by the Buddha in terms of the 'four noble truths' – a formulation of the Dharma that applies the principle of conditionality to the whole of conditioned existence, including both samsara and the path to nirvana.

technical terms in Buddhism

noble truths

The Pali expression usually translated as 'noble truths' is *ariya-saccāni*. But a *sacca* is a 'reality' as well as a 'truth'. In addition, *ariya-saccāni* is a compound that has various meanings built in to its grammar. As well as 'noble truths or realities', it could mean 'truths or realities which are ennobling'; it could also mean 'truths or realities which are taught by the noble one (i.e. the Buddha)', or 'the truths or realities taught by the noble ones (i.e. by all Buddhas, all awakened beings)'. So *ariya-saccāni* might also have been translated as 'those ennobling realities taught by the Buddha' – *dukkha*, its origin, its cessation, and the path leading to its cessation.

The doctrine of the four noble truths might be the most famous teaching of the Buddha, and is traditionally regarded as having been taught by the Buddha in his First Sermon. Having become awakened on the banks of the Nerañjarā river, the Buddha made his way several hundred miles to the Deer Park in Sarnath near Benares, because he wanted to share his discovery of awakening with his five former companions living there.[10] Here, then, is the account of the noble truths as given by the Buddha to those first disciples:

> Monks, this is the noble truth of *dukkha*: birth is *dukkha*, ageing is *dukkha*, sickness is *dukkha*, association with the unloved is *dukkha*, separation from the loved is *dukkha*, not getting what one wants is *dukkha*; in short, the five masses (*khandhas*) of clinging are *dukkha*.
>
> Monks, this is the noble truth of the origin of *dukkha*: the craving for further existence that goes together with greed and delight, the taking pleasure now here, now there – namely, craving for sense-pleasures, craving for existence, craving for non-existence.
>
> Monks, this is the noble truth of the cessation of *dukkha*: the cessation and fading away without remainder of that very craving – giving it up, letting it go, being freed, unseated from it.
>
> Monks, this is the noble truth of the practice leading to the cessation of *dukkha*: just this eightfold path, namely, right view, right intention, right speech, right action, right livelihood, right effort, right mindfulness, right concentration.[11]

The principle of conditionality can be seen at work in this formula of the four noble truths. First, there is *dukkha*; second, this *dukkha* arises with craving as its origin; therefore, third, it ceases with the cessation of craving; and, fourth, the way to that ceasing is by practising the eightfold path. In formulating the four noble truths the Buddha was applying his principle of conditionality to the basic problem of human experience, so as to share the solution he had discovered. Hence, they are also 'realities taught by the noble one': four aspects of how things really are, as seen from the perspective of awakening.[12]

Nicely enough, however, it seems as though this application of conditionality was designed to look like a medical diagnosis, with the implication that the Buddha's Dharma is a medicine to heal the disease of *dukkha*.[13] The first truth states the problem, that is, the disease or symptom – it is *dukkha*: all the difficulty, pain and unsatisfactoriness that we experience. The second truth states the origin (*samudaya*) of *dukkha*, that is, the diagnosis – it is *taṇhā* or craving. Hence, on condition of craving arises *dukkha*. But since this *dukkha* has a condition, then with the cessation of that condition, the *dukkha* will cease. Hence, the third truth states the solution or prognosis – that there is a cessation (*nirodha*) of *dukkha* – so the prognosis is good. The fourth truth states the cure for *dukkha*, the way (*magga*) to bring about the cessation of craving – it is the noble eightfold path.

***Dukkha* and its origin in craving**

The four noble truths fall into two parts: (i) there is *dukkha*, and its origin is craving; and (ii) there is the cessation of *dukkha* through the cessation of craving, and the eightfold path is the way to this cessation. Arising and ceasing – this is the essence of the Dharma as taught to Sāriputta by Assaji. Let us consider, however, what it might mean to say that everything that is problematic in life arises with craving as its condition. Would it not make more sense to put it the other way round: that it is craving that arises with *dukkha* as its condition? Surely, it is pain and unsatisfactoriness that cause our various desires and obsessions? It would seem to be a common-sense view that all of our different cravings are attempts to assuage various kinds of suffering in our experience – and that sometimes they are quite successful. After dancing for several hours, for instance, I feel acutely thirsty; and then water tastes good. If I have been working hard, I need a holiday; and two weeks on the beach will renew me in body and mind.

The Buddha's teaching, however, is concerned with the underlying *dukkha* of the human situation, which is there even after a good dance and a relaxing holiday. We have characterized the problematic nature of existence by describing the reactive mind, with its tendency to slip into automatic and default habitual modes. This is part of what the term 'craving' is supposed to suggest. The word translates the Pali term *taṇhā*, which literally means 'thirst'. This vivid metaphor is used to sum up our often unconscious, embodied desire for satisfaction, for satisfying sensual experiences or for a satisfying sense of being a really existing person or ego. It is craving that gets us on the move, looking for enjoyment, for escape, for ourselves. None of this is necessarily a bad thing; after all, the spiritual life itself begins with a desire for deeper meaning, and we may feel a great passion for the Dharma. But Sangharakshita describes more typical experiences of craving like this:

> When we are experiencing craving we want something, anything – something to read, someone to talk to, something to eat – that will fill that gap, mop up that moment of discomfort. In the grip of craving, we wolf down our food to keep misery, shame and emptiness at bay, or try to snatch happiness from sex or power or money to assuage our aching emptiness. We can even have a craving for meditative states, looking for quick results and getting impatient when they don't materialise. We crave company, looking to other people to make us happy, using them to plug the gap in our positivity. We crave annihilation, even, imagining that oblivion will solve our problems. The object of craving is not the issue: craving is craving . . . The discomfort of neurotic attachment, itself produced by craving, produces further craving. In order to break this vicious circle it is therefore necessary, at least at the start of our spiritual life, to be prepared simply to experience that craving, or stifled energy, or inner void, and not try to satisfy it or release it or fill it.[14]

Sangharakshita draws our attention to two important aspects of *taṇhā* or craving. First, what we mean by the craving that leads to *dukkha* is the reaction to existence as unsatisfactory. So craving is related to *dukkha*, but it makes it much worse. Second, he draws attention to the necessity to experience this craving for what it is. The exercise of simple awareness marks the shift from an absorption in the reactive mode to the beginnings of creative awareness. Our craving is usually itself based on unawareness, but by doing something as simple as breaking the flow of unthinking desire, we open up the path that leads to the end of craving.

Cessation and the path

This recognition of craving as craving might come in the form of disgust. I used to buy more books than I was ever likely to read. My craving for books seemed fine – after all, it came from a 'thirst for knowledge'. However, this craving betrayed itself as not entirely worthy. Browsing in a bookshop, I would get excited by the idea of reading certain books, and learning about unknown new things; I would buy books, but then not actually read them, since new ideas and more books would soon attract my attention. Once I went on a long solitary retreat in Scotland. Travelling home, I called into a bookshop in Edinburgh, and was soon queuing to pay for four or five new books. Then I realized with a start that what I was doing was a travesty of the life of meditation and contentment I had been cultivating in the previous weeks. I put the books back and caught the train home. I realized that this craving for books was really no different from any other gorging or materialist excess; it was just another way to avoid how life really feels. Now I have a useful strategy for buying books: if I notice a desirable book, I wait until the next day before buying it. The delay allows restraint and thoughtfulness to arise; I buy far fewer books these days.

Recognizing craving for what it is means less neurotic, automatic, or habitual behaviour; hence the gradual reduction and ceasing of craving. Talk of 'cessation', the third noble truth, might give the impression that the Buddhist path is concerned with a life-denying negation of human passion, but this is more a problem of translation. The Pali word *nirodha* has a broad connotation; although it sometimes does mean 'cessation' as the opposite of 'arising', in the context of the *nirodha* of conditions that give rise to samsara it means 'ceasing to be a problem' rather than 'ceasing to exist'. It is when conditions that give rise to *dukkha* cease to be a problem that suffering ceases to be a problem for us.[15] This is largely a matter of changing the way we approach life, shifting from the reactive to the creative mode; this does not mean denying life, but means finding the deeper springs from which life flows. This shift is what living out the Buddhist path involves.[16]

However, the craving that troubles us is not only of a personal and psychological sort. As we have seen, the word *taṇhā* points to an underlying tendency that belongs not just to human nature but perhaps to the nature of life itself: it is the craving for pleasure and satisfaction that unconsciously shapes our whole outlook and expectations. There is no question of somehow getting rid of this kind of passion, hard-wired, as it were, into humanity. The path consists rather of gradually seeing desire for what it is, and letting go through insight. Since this task itself involves a kind of passion for truth and for liberation, it is a matter of desire transformed through spiritual practice; or, in Buddhist terms, of *kāma-chanda*, desire for sensual pleasure, transmuted by and into *dhamma-chanda*, desire for the truth.[17]

With the cessation of craving, *dukkha* ceases to be a problem: this is the practical conclusion to the Buddha's teaching. But this does not mean that awakened beings experience no pain. Even the Buddha experienced physical pain. As an old man he said this to his attendant, Ānanda:

> Ānanda, I am now old, elderly and at the end of my life; I have reached eighty years old. Just as a decrepit cart keeps going with makeshift repairs, likewise, Ānanda, the *tathāgata*'s body seems to keep going with makeshift repairs. Only when the *tathāgata*, through the cessation of certain feelings, and from not paying attention to outer

> signs, enters and abides in a signless concentration of mind, it is only then that his body is more comfortable.[18]

Even the Buddha experienced the aches and pains of old age, and only found relief in meditation. This suggests that the Buddhist path leads to *dukkha* ceasing to be a problem rather than to some magical disappearance of all physical pain.

This important teaching is illustrated in a discourse called 'The Arrow'. The Buddha first describes how an ordinary unawakened person reacts to pain:

> Monks, when an uninformed ordinary person is touched by painful feeling, that person cries, distressed and distraught, with breast-beating and wailing, confusion and collapse. That person feels two feelings, one physical and one emotional. Suppose, monks, someone was shot with an arrow, and then shot again with a second arrow: such a person will feel the pain of both arrows. Likewise, monks, an uninformed ordinary person, touched by painful feeling, cries, distressed and distraught, with breast-beating and wailing, confusion and collapse. That person feels two feelings, one physical and one emotional.[19]

This 'second arrow' is our secondary emotional reaction to physical pain: we commonly react by averting from pain, or by seeking relief in pleasant sensual experience, or by taking refuge in unawareness. All this is included in what the Buddha meant by craving as a reaction to experience. He went on to describe the response of an awakened person to painful feeling:

> When an informed noble disciple is touched by painful feeling, that person does not cry, and is not distressed and distraught, and there is no breast-beating and wailing, confusion or collapse. That person feels a single feeling that is physical, not emotional. Suppose, monks, someone was shot with an arrow, but not shot again with a second arrow: such a person will feel the pain of a single arrow. Likewise, monks, an informed noble

> disciple, touched by painful feeling, does not cry, is not distressed and distraught, and there is no breast-beating and wailing, confusion or collapse. That person feels a single feeling that is physical, not emotional.[20]

Someone without craving still feels physical pain as pain, but by not reacting to it, they experience freedom from the 'second arrow' of reaction.[21] The end of *dukkha,* therefore, does not mean the end of all physical pain. It refers rather to such pain ceasing to be a problem because one does not react to it with aversion.

Mindful awareness and the 'gap'

Most of us, most of the time, believe that the solution to life's problems consists in having more of what gives us pleasure and less of what gives us pain. This reactive strategy of rejecting pain and seeking pleasure happens so naturally it is mostly unconscious, but it also keeps us relentlessly seeking pleasure in a world often characterized by pain and change. So the wheel of samsara continues, and our experience arises on various conditions in an endless cycle of reaction. The Buddhist path offers a completely different way of finding a more satisfying life. We can gain a taste of this way of freedom right away by attending with mindful awareness to our experience. Awareness has none of the excitement of sensual stimulation, and none of the exhaustion and disappointment either. Its pleasures are non-sensual, those of peace and sanity in the midst of events, and also that of nearing the source of life, that inner spring of the creative mind. The Buddha described this awareness as the way to the Deathless:

> Heedful awareness is the way to the deathless state;
> Heedlessness is the way to death.
> Those who are heedful will not die,
> But those who are heedless are like the dead.[22]

Mindful awareness enables us to move from the reactive to the creative mode of functioning. To use a metaphor, this awareness is a 'gap' between feeling and craving, and is one of the conditions on which the Buddhist path becomes possible. Once the Buddha was approached by Māluṅkyaputta – the same monk whom the Buddha had compared to someone wounded with a poisoned arrow. But Māluṅkyaputta had long given up his concern for speculative metaphysics. Now he was an old monk, and he asked the Buddha for some brief teaching on which to meditate. The Buddha asked him whether he ever wanted things that he did not already have, to which Māluṅkyaputta answered that he did not: he was obviously an experienced Dharma practitioner. Then the Buddha gave him this powerful short teaching:

> For you then, Māluṅkyaputta, as regards things seen, heard, sensed, or perceived, there will be in the seen only the seen, in the heard only the heard, in the sensed only the sensed, and in the perceived only the perceived. When for you, Māluṅkyaputta, as regards things seen, heard, sensed, or perceived, there will be in the seen only the seen, in the heard only the heard, in the sensed only the sensed, and in the perceived only the perceived, then who you are, Māluṅkyaputta, will not be defined by that. When who you are, Māluṅkyaputta, is not defined by that, then who you are will not be found in that. When who you are, Māluṅkyaputta, is not found in that, then who you are is neither here, nor in the beyond, nor in between. Just this is the end of *dukkha*.[23]

This brief, dense teaching recommends complete attentiveness to present experience, and the consequent liberation from any limiting sense of self.

A characteristic part of life in samsara is our constant identification with our own thoughts, our own story about 'who we are'. This ceaseless narrative can be so pervasive that we barely notice it, like a fish that does not notice the water through which it constantly moves and on which it depends. It is this narrative about the self that provides the warm atmosphere in which craving and aversion lives. Let's say my friend fails to greet me on the street. I feel hurt, and I start thinking about how he doesn't like me and why I don't care. So I don't ring him up, and it's only much later, after much quite unnecessary upset, that I discover he had simply not noticed me, having just had some bad news. The Buddha's brief teaching to Māluṅkyaputta invited him into an awareness in which all such thoughts are seen just for what they are – just thoughts.

Māluṅkyaputta goes on to put the Buddha's brief teaching into verses he has himself composed, which the Buddha then repeats to indicate that he approves of them. These verses give us another perspective on awareness, on how it leads to lightness and non-clinging around enjoyable experiences:

> Seeing something lovely, attentive to attractiveness,
> one's awareness gets confused.
> Experiencing it with a heart of delight, one carries on relishing it.
> Many feelings for it increase, all arising from that lovely thing.
> One's mind then becomes harmed by coveting and ill will;
> so *dukkha* is heaped up, and nirvana said to be far away.
>
> Seeing something lovely, but ever mindful, one does not delight in it.
> Experiencing it with a detached heart, one does not keep on relishing.
> The mindful person practises by letting go, not by heaping up;
> and though one sees every lovely thing, and fully feels each feeling,
> *dukkha* is not heaped up, and nirvana is said to be very near.[24]

Māluṅkyaputta's verses, we should notice, are not recommending that we avoid all enjoyment and sensual pleasure. Rather, they point out how lack of awareness means that we envelop enjoyable experience with craving. Perhaps we see a lovely sunset; but instead of enjoying it with a heart informed by awareness, the experience becomes something to photograph, hold onto, boast about, or regret not having more of. Being aware can only increase wholesome aspects of enjoyment.

The idea that we stop being caught up in the endless business of seeking pleasure and avoiding pain, and that we step back to examine the whole matter – this message will always seem a little dissonant. It might take us some time to appreciate how the practice of awareness and the cultivation of the Buddhist path will help us, because the truth of conditionality is hard to see and to understand. Even Sāriputta and Moggallāna, who came quickly to a vision of conditionality as leading from *dukkha* to the Deathless, had subsequently to practise the Dharma in order to internalize and realize their vision of the truth. But because the very nature of the path is to lead away from *dukkha*, every step has the relish of liberation.

Questions for Chapter Two

1. Sāriputta was clearly very excited by what he heard about the Dharma from Assaji, more so than by anything he had heard from other teachers. Is there any aspect of the Dharma that particularly excites you?
2. What are the characteristics of the reactive mind and what are the characteristics of the creative mind?
3. The second of the four noble truths teaches that craving is the origin of *dukkha*. How do you experience craving in your life? What conditions lead you to experience more craving? You may like to draw a diagram to show them, and the relationships between these conditions.
4. Reflect on what conditions might help you to maintain a creative mind in the face of the tendency towards craving. Does meditation help? Draw a diagram to show how these conditions work. How do they compare to the noble eightfold path?
5. Write down some ways of completing the following sentence: 'I am a person who . . . .' Are you always that way? With everyone? Everywhere? To the same degree? Notice how it feels when you notice that something you have said about yourself is not always true.

Chapter Three

The Twelve Links

In Chapter Two we saw how the Buddha's teaching of the four noble truths applies the principle of conditionality to the arising and the ceasing of *dukkha*. In this chapter I will explore the teaching of the twelve *nidānas*, or 'links', of *paṭicca-samuppāda*, which the Buddha taught to explain in detail the arising of *dukkha*. This chapter will not make for cheerful reading, because we will be stripping back the false comforts of samsara and conducting an anatomy of the reactive mind. But I will balance things up in Chapter Four by exploring the dependent arising of the path to liberation and happiness.

The twelve *nidānas* in the Pali canon

If you read books on Buddhism, you will probably find yourself reading that the Buddha taught the twelve links, or *nidānas*, of *paṭicca-samuppāda*. Later Buddhist writers in fact very often identified the twelve links with *paṭicca-samuppāda*. In this book, however, I understand the twelvefold list only as a particularly important application of the principle of conditionality, detailing the very structure, as it were, of unawakened human experience. In the Pali discourses the Buddha is described as meditating on the twelve *nidānas* immediately after his awakening:

> Thus have I heard. Once the Blessed One was living at Uruvelā, on the bank of the Nerañjarā river, at the root of the Bodhi tree, just after he had become fully awakened. Now at that time the Blessed One sat cross-legged for seven days experiencing the bliss of liberation. Then at the end of those seven days, the Blessed One emerged

> from that meditative concentration and in the first watch of the night paid close attention to dependent arising (*paṭicca-samuppāda*) in forward order, in this way:
>
> 'This being, that becomes; from the arising of this, that arises; this not being, that does not become; from the ceasing of this, that ceases, namely – dependent on ignorance arise formations; dependent on formations arises consciousness; dependent on consciousness arises name-and-form; dependent on name-and-form arise the six sense realms; dependent on the six sense realms arises contact; dependent on contact arises feeling; dependent on feeling arises craving; dependent on craving arises clinging; dependent on clinging arises existence; dependent on existence arises birth; dependent on birth arises old age and death, grief, sorrow, pain, misery, and despair. Thus is the arising of this whole mass of *dukkha*.
>
> 'But from the fading away and cessation without remainder of just this ignorance, formations cease; from the cessation of formations, consciousness ceases; from the cessation of consciousness, name-and-form cease; from the cessation of name-and-form, the six sense realms cease; from the cessation of the six sense realms, contact ceases; from the cessation of contact, feeling ceases; from the cessation of feeling, craving ceases; from the cessation of craving, clinging ceases; from the cessation of clinging, existence ceases; from the cessation of existence, birth ceases; from the cessation of birth, old age and death, grief, sorrow, pain, misery, and despair cease. Thus is the cessation of this whole mass of *dukkha*.'[1]

The discourse describes an occasion in the Buddha's life not long after he had gained awakening. He was sitting under the Bodhi tree, enjoying the bliss that had come from his liberation. After a week of this, he thought about what exactly

technical terms in Buddhism

nidāna

(the same in Pali and Sanskrit). We usually translate this word as 'link', talking of the 'twelve links' of *paṭicca-samuppāda* or dependent arising, but the word *nidāna* means more than this. It's an ancient Vedic word meaning a 'tie', a rope used as a halter for an animal. The Buddhist use of the word is more abstract, and it can mean the 'source', the 'foundation' or the 'cause' of something. When the Buddhist teachings say that feeling is the *nidāna* for craving, for instance, they mean that feeling is the source, the foundation, and the cause of craving. In this sense a *nidāna* is also an explanation or reason, and the twelve *nidānas* are twelve explanations of or reasons why human beings experience *dukkha*.

had happened in the process of his awakening; the twelve links represent the whole samsaric process that in him had now been utterly quenched. He ran over in his mind how the twelve links, representing all of samsara, had arisen, but also how they had ceased, such that, with his awakening, the 'whole mass' of his *dukkha* had come to an end.

What do these twelve links mean? Unfortunately the ancient records of the Buddha's teaching do not preserve a clear and unambiguous explanation of how to interpret the twelvefold series. In this chapter I will present two ways of looking at them. The first one is the traditional Buddhist interpretation of the twelve *nidānas*, which understands them as explaining the rebirth process as it occurs over three lifetimes. However, while this interpretation has been worked out over many centuries in the Buddhist tradition, it is not to be found in the early Buddhist teachings, which mainly present the twelve links just as explaining the arising and the ceasing of *dukkha*. In this chapter I will first briefly present the three-life interpretation, but then at greater length present the *nidānas* as applying to human experience in the present life.[2]

The Wheel of Life and the three-life interpretation

The traditional way of understanding the twelve *nidānas* is illustrated in a series of pictures set around the outside of the famous Buddhist image of the *bhavacakra* or 'Wheel of Life'. To this day, huge pictures of the *bhavacakra* are to be found in the entrance halls of Tibetan Buddhist temples, presenting devotees with a vivid reminder of samsara. The symbol did not arise until several centuries after the time of the Buddha, but encapsulates many Buddhist teachings in one complicated representation. The Buddhist tradition takes it for granted that all living beings will be reborn according to their karma. This process of rebirth is said to have no discernible beginning; according to this world view it is the fate of every living thing to revolve endlessly in the Wheel of Life until they escape through individual spiritual effort.[3] While many Buddhists hold this view of life quite literally, it is also possible to regard it as a powerfully explanatory story, the objective truth of which is hard to know; a story that can be understood as applying from moment to moment as well as across lifetimes.

The Wheel of Life should be seen as a representation of how human beings create their own destiny. The god of death, Yama, symbolizing impermanence, holds up a huge mirror in his talons – in which we see the situation we are all in. Reflected in the mirror is our world of experience in the form of an endlessly revolving wheel. At its centre a cockerel, representing greed, chases a snake, representing hate, which chases a pig, representing delusion, which chases the cockerel. These three beasts, representing the three root defilements, symbolize the largely unconscious forces that dominate the reactive mind and lead to ever-renewed *dukkha*. Around this hub of the Wheel are two segments, white and black. In the white segment, beings move upwards, their positive and wholesome actions accompanied by happy and rewarding states of existence. In the black segment, beings fall downwards, their negative and unwholesome actions dragging them into miserable and ugly compensations.

Surrounding the centre of the Wheel are the six realms of rebirth for living beings: the heavenly realm of the long-lived

Figure 2: *The 'Wheel of Life', a mirror reflecting all of samsara held in the claws of the god of death. (© Aloka.)*

gods (*devas*), the titanic realm of the competitive demons (*asuras*), the frustrating realm of the hungry ghosts (*pretas*), the terrible realm of punishing hells, the repetitive realm of the instinctual animals, and the realm of human beings. These realms can also be understood as metaphors for psychological states. We can be sitting in the same room as someone who is experiencing terrible mental and emotional pain, in a psychic hell, while we ourselves are enjoying a heavenly time as a result of previous wholesome actions – or vice versa.

These realms of rebirth, or psychic states, arise on conditions, illustrated by the twelve pictures around the outside of the Wheel of Life representing the twelve links of *paṭicca-samuppāda*. The twelve links illustrate the detailed process by which beings take rebirth, now in blissful states, now in painful ones, as a consequence of the ethical quality of their actions.

(i) The first link is *ignorance.* This is represented by a blind person feeling their way forward – the situation of living beings who are not aware of the Dharma and do not comprehend the human situation as it really is. Instead, they blunder along in existence, stuck in the reactive mode because of wrong views and unhelpful attitudes.

(ii) The second picture shows a potter making pots. This is a representation of *formations*, usually understood as *karma* or *volitional formations*. Our habitual activities, our decisions informed by ignorance, are like constructions that fix us into definite ways of being.

(iii) The third link is *consciousness*, pictured as a monkey in a flowering tree. This consciousness has arisen dependent on a previous life, and is once more ready to swing from branch to branch, ever looking for fresh pleasures, which we continue to think might satisfy 'me', the conscious ego.

(iv) The fourth picture shows some people in a boat, travelling along. This is a representation of *name-and-form*, which is a Buddhist way of talking about the person, envisaged as a mind (the rowers) and a body (the boat) joined together. Now we believe that we *are* this body and mind.

(v) The fifth link is *the six sense realms*, represented as a house with five windows and a door. This is the human person – a house, with experience coming and going via the five senses plus the mind considered as a sixth sense. All experience comes through the six senses.

(vi) The sixth picture shows a couple kissing; this represents *contact* between one of the sense-bases and an object. Our immediate present experience is a matter of contact between consciousness and the world via the senses.

(vii) The seventh link is the *feeling* that arises from contact, represented as someone with an arrow in his or her eye. Although this image suggests unmitigated pain, feeling can be pleasant, painful, or neutral. Life always feels a certain way – good, bad, or indifferent.

(viii) The eighth picture shows a seated man being offered a drink by a woman; this represents *thirst* – the craving for more pleasure, or to be rid of pain, that arises on condition of feeling. This is the craving that nourishes the reactive mind, ever searching for satisfaction.

(ix) The ninth link is the *clinging* that follows from craving, here pictured as someone gathering fruit from a tree – holding on to sensual experience, or to views, beliefs, and habits; getting attached to things that are not really constant. This clinging is the way we try to make our lives workable.

(x) The tenth picture shows a pregnant woman, representing the *existence* or *becoming* that follows from clinging – the new life within her symbolizes the continuity of existence across rebirths when there is grasping. This continuity applies in this life too: moments of craving and clinging are pregnant with consequences.

(xi) The eleventh link is *birth*, and it is represented quite literally as the birth of a baby, with all the pain, blood, and sweat involved. But anything that has been born must inevitably die.

(xii) The twelfth and last picture shows a dead body being carried on someone's back, presumably towards a cemetery, and this represents *old age and death* – the inevitable consequence of birth.

Hence arises this whole mass of suffering. The illustrations of the twelve links, we should note, are representations designed to make the teaching memorable. The pictures, like the image of the Wheel of Life itself, were not taught by the Buddha, but arose in the Buddhist tradition several centuries after the Buddha's time, as generations of Buddhists considered how to understand and present the Dharma. The most important source for the way the twelve links are understood in the Wheel of Life is that of the philosophical tradition known as Abhidharma.

In the systematic analysis of the Abhidharma, the twelve *nidānas* are presented as explaining the rebirth process over three successive lives.[4] In this interpretation the twelve links are taken to represent a series of stages in the unfolding of an individual's life. *Ignorance* and *formations* describe the karma of the previous existence that is the cause of the present life. *Consciousness* is the resultant linking element between these existences, appearing in the mother's womb when conditions are appropriate. *Name-and-form* refer to the new body and mind of the embryo, which then develops the *six sense spheres* as it matures inside and beyond the womb. Having been born, the new being experiences *contact* and *feeling* as he or she encounters the world. All this is the result of the past karma that has led to present existence. But now, with present *feeling*, there is *craving* in the moment – new and active volitions that are the karma of the present life. *Clinging* and *existence* are also active volitional forces, leading to *birth* and *ageing-and-death*, the results of all this karma in a further existence.

The three-life interpretation is therefore an explanation of how the rebirth process happens, and of how further existence on the Wheel of Life will come about. This interpretation of the *nidānas* is very widely accepted among traditional Buddhists.[5] It can perhaps be best presented in a table:[6]

nidāna	**explanation**		**lifetime**
avijjā	ignorance	**karma**-process	*previous life*
saṅkhārā	volitional formations		
viññāṇa	consciousness: the re-linking (*paṭisandhi*) consciousness between lives	**result-** (*vipāka*) process	*present life*
nāma-rūpa	name-and-form: mind and body arising at conception in this life		
saḷāyatanāni	the six sense organs in the embryo		
phassa	contact with the world		
vedanā	feeling		
taṇhā	craving	**karma**-process	
upādāna	clinging		
bhava	existence in samsara		
jāti	birth in the next life	**result**-process	*next life*
jarā-maraṇa	old age and death in the next life		

The twelve *nidānas* as explaining *dukkha*

Although taking the twelve links as applying over three lifetimes is the traditional way of interpreting the *nidānas*, it is not in fact found in the Pali discourses. Instead, the Buddha taught the *nidānas* as twelve interconnected ways in which *dukkha* arises, and in what follows I will try to bring out the meaning of each of the *nidānas* in relation to *dukkha*. It must be said that the Buddha's teaching here is by no means easy to understand; he is explaining the process by which human beings become entangled in samsara. Before we go into this interpretation, there are two points to bear in mind. Firstly, the scheme of twelve *nidānas* is perhaps best regarded as a mnemonic, that is, a convenient list to be memorized for the purposes of reflection. There are, in fact, several different versions of the *nidāna* chain, with six, nine, or ten items, though the version with twelve has become the standard one.[7] Secondly, by putting aside the three-life interpretation of the twelve *nidānas*, I am not claiming that the Buddha did not teach rebirth, as he did teach it.[8] However, the interpretation of the twelve *nidānas* as explaining *dukkha* makes sense whether or not you believe in rebirth.[9]

There is an important clue about how to understand the twelve links in a discourse called 'Contemplation of the Pairs'. In this discourse the Buddha examines each one of the *nidānas* in turn and describes how it should be contemplated as the condition upon which *dukkha* arises, so that with the cessation of this *nidāna*, there is a cessation of suffering:

> Whatever *dukkha* arises, all of it has ignorance [or formations, or consciousness, and so on] as its condition... from the fading away and cessation without remainder of just this ignorance [or formations, or consciousness, and so on] there is no arising of *dukkha*.[10]

In the teaching of the four noble truths the Buddha explained that craving is the origin of *dukkha*; now we also see how this craving is not the only condition on which everything problematic in life arises, but just the most important. There are other conditions, especially ignorance, which sustain *dukkha*. In the Buddha's more complete teaching on *dukkha* we discover that suffering arises in a complex matrix of conditions, of which the Buddha especially highlighted twelve.

Not only do the twelve *nidānas* show how *dukkha* arises through twelve interconnected conditions; those conditions are also ordered in a linear sequence that shows the dynamic of human existence. As long as there is ignorance, there arises the sense of 'I' and 'me' as separate from the world. With this separation, this 'I' experiences this world, perceiving it, reacting to it by feelings of liking or not liking, and hence developing craving and aversion towards it. Hence the reactive mind is born, and it develops as a 'someone' who clings to what 'he' or 'she' knows, existing as this person that 'I' think I am. And hence I am someone who is 'born', and therefore it is inevitable that 'I' will age and die. However, with the ceasing of ignorance, this whole sequence of conditions ceases. Without ignorance, the sense of there being a fixed sense of 'I' and 'me' ceases. There is instead the spontaneity of the creative mind, open to experiencing what happens with awareness and positivity. This is the 'unconditioned' state, which is 'unborn' and therefore not prone to 'ageing and death'. This is the Deathless that Sāriputta and Moggallāna discovered through encountering the teaching of conditionality, and it is a state of complete human fulfillment.

The sequence of links, with birth, ageing and death depending on a whole series of cognitive and psychological conditions, suggests that our usual experience of life, and our familiar sense of being a self or an ego, is a conditioned structure, like a house. Although such a structure apparently provides safety, security, and definition, it is also fixed, limited, and resistant to change. The Buddha's discovery was that the taking down of this 'house' of the ordinary ego is the way to the end of *dukkha*. Ignorance and craving are the 'builders' of the house, and when they cease to function in their blind and reactive ways, the conditions that hold up the structure of *dukkha* are gone, and the 'house' of unsatisfactory experience collapses. Although this might sound disastrous, the dismantling of the usual structure of experience is the way to liberation and the way out of reactive mental functioning. The Buddha expressed this poetical way of thinking about what it means for the *nidānas* to cease in his famous 'Song of Victory', traditionally regarded as uttered just after his awakening:

> I have run through countless lives
> of wandering and not finding
> the house-builder that I sought –
> rebirth is pain and yet more pain!

But, house-builder, you are seen:
you will not build this house again.
Every rafter now is broken
and the ridgepole taken down;
mind unfabricated, open,
and craving left behind.[11]

The images of the 'house' and the 'house-builder' allow us a poetic approach to how samsara has arisen on conditions: through our spiritual ignorance and our craving for existence, we have built the 'house' of our sense of self, of 'me' and 'mine'. But nevertheless this 'house' is not a safe refuge from the vicissitudes of existence, for it is only a temporary structure that cannot long endure when there is damp and dry rot, and which needs much maintenance as the events of life batter at it. By contrast, the Dharma is an invitation into creative freedom.

The Buddhist teaching is therefore an invitation to stop building. The practice of awareness, when undertaken as part of the Buddhist path, allows us to let go of those house-builders, ignorance and craving, that are the foundation of the reactive mind. We experience a gradual freeing up of creativity and positivity, and discover, against the grain of what we might expect, that we can function perfectly well as a human being without the limiting security of a fixed sense of self. But before we consider the path (in Chapter Four), let us study the twelve links in more detail.

Ignorance, formations, consciousness, and name-and-form

'**Ignorance**' (in Pali, *avijjā*, in Sanskrit, *avidyā*) is defined in the suttas in a somewhat technical way: as not knowing about *dukkha*, not knowing about the origin of *dukkha*, not knowing about the cessation of *dukkha*, and not knowing about the path that leads to the cessation of *dukkha*. This means, in short, not knowing the four noble truths. Since the four truths are themselves an application of the principle of conditionality, ignorance therefore means not knowing about how experience arises on particular conditions – a lack of insight or wisdom in the Buddhist sense. Sangharakshita provides us with a more poetic description of this ignorance:

> *Avidyā* is not ignorance in the intellectual sense, so much as a lack or deprivation of spiritual awareness – even of spiritual consciousness and spiritual being. *Avidyā* in this sense is the direct antithesis of *Bodhi*, Enlightenment... If Enlightenment represents the goal, then ignorance represents the depths from which we have come. If Enlightenment represents the mountain peak, then ignorance represents the valleys from which we are gradually emerging and which lie wrapped in darkness.[12]

Ignorance is not to be regarded, however, as a quasi-cosmic principle upon which all life is based. The Buddha taught that, although no beginning of the ignorance that gives rise to samsara can be perceived, it too arises on particular conditions – on unwholesome actions of body, speech, and mind. In this sense, the *dukkha* of the present life is the result of past ignorance that was itself constantly sustained by unethical actions. This ignorance is not, therefore, just cognitive or intellectual. The unwholesome roots (*akusala-mūlas*) of greed, hate, and delusion are both emotional and cognitive, being those deep-seated tendencies that find expression in unwholesome actions, speech, and thoughts. In more contemporary terms, they represent the unregenerate side of human nature – no doubt a part of humanity's evolutionary inheritance, but now evident in such obviously negative activities as suicide bombing, the use of nuclear weapons, and the reckless destruction of natural habitats.

This ignorance continues to manifest as an active force in how we go about living. The beliefs and views that people hold, which inform how they make decisions and go about their lives, are often based on unawareness. Ritualistic religious beliefs, the idea that certain practices like bathing or fasting can be ethically purifying, for instance, are ignorant views, from the Buddhist point of view. The belief in a God on whom we depend and who will look after us is an ignorant belief too, corresponding to the projection of authority and power onto an imagined deity. From the Buddhist point of view such a belief only makes it harder to take responsibility for our well-being – it is a form of spiritual immaturity.

The **'formations'** (in Pali, *saṅkhāras*, in Sanskrit, *saṃskāras*) that arise dependent on ignorance are defined as bodily formations, verbal formations, and mental formations. These refer to those actions of body, speech, and mind that follow unthinkingly from unawareness. If ignorance is compared to the state of being drunk, then the formations are like the things we do when we are intoxicated. We laugh, we cry, we bemoan our lot and fantasize about our future – all while we are more or less befuddled by the confusions of basic unawareness.

Formations refer to the dispositions, habits, and tendencies that make up a human personality, going along in his or her familiar pattern of life. The formations are connected with the law of karma in that it is the repetition of intentional actions that sets up our ingrained personality traits and habits (I will explore these matters in Chapter Five). Of course, there are good habits as well as bad; we are more concerned here with the negative. Formations are the basic patterns of the reactive mind: the stock of fallback behaviours that we rely upon in times of need; a set of strategies that get us through difficult moments, before we can relax into our more comfortable habits. In contemporary terms, these formations represent unexplored and unresolved emotions and tendencies that often keep us revolving in painfully limited experiences.

Ignorance and formations are traditionally interpreted as the karma-process of a previous existence: the factors on condition of which this life came about. We can also understand these first two links as the general background conditions of experience: while there is ignorance and the ingrained habits of personality, our tendency will be to live out of the reactive mind, to repeat unhelpful kinds of behaviour, and to cause difficulties for ourselves and for others.

The **'consciousness'** (in Pali, *viññāṇa*, in Sanskrit, *vijñāna*) that arises dependent on ignorance and formations is the divided sense of being a 'subject' who is separate from experience. This consciousness is a source of *dukkha* when we assume that there is a self or person who is 'behind' our sense-experiences. This was the kind of assumption made by the Buddha's contemporaries who believed in the *ātman*, or permanent Self, which transmigrated between lives. This assumption leads us to seek salvation in spiritual experiences or by looking forward to a pure heaven realm after death. The Buddha also taught rebirth, but no *ātman* that is reborn; there is just a continuity of conditioned processes. The emphasis of the Buddha's teaching was instead to look at the conditions upon which bondage and liberation arise in the here and now. Ultimately, as he taught Māluṅkyaputta, there is 'in the seen just the seen, in the heard just the heard', and so on.

The **'name-and-form'** (in both Pali and Sanskrit, *nāma-rūpa*) that is dependent on consciousness is a way of describing the psychophysical organism. 'Form' (*rūpa*) is defined as that which consists of the four great elements, that is to say, earth (solidity), water (cohesion), air (movement), and fire (temperature); the objective component of what we are, meaning our physical bodies as we experience them. Name (*nāma*) is defined as feeling, perception, volition, contact, and attention; that is to say, mind as an active process, the way the mind works. Name-and-form is a source of *dukkha* when we suppose that our minds and bodies are who we really are. This assumption is more or less the opposite of supposing that we are really the pure consciousness that lies behind our experience. Thinking that we are really just our physical bodies is a form of materialism; thinking that we are really pure consciousness is a kind of spiritualism or idealism.

The Buddha's Dharma upsets both these kinds of assumption by teaching that consciousness and name-and-form arise dependent on each other, and cannot exist one without the other. Sāriputta once talked about this with another senior disciple, Mahākoṭṭhita, and compared this interdependence to that of two sheaves of reeds leaning upon each other:

> My friend, I will make you a comparison, because some intelligent people understand better through

> similes what the teachings mean. Friend, it is as if two sheaves of reeds were stood leaning upon each other. Likewise, consciousness exists with name-and-form as its condition, and name-and-form exists with consciousness as its condition. With name-and-form as their condition are the six sense realms, with the six sense realms as condition is contact ... Thus there is the arising of this whole mass of suffering. If one of these sheaves of reeds were to be pulled away, the other would fall over; if the other were to be pulled away, the first would fall over. Likewise, from the cessation of name-and-form is the cessation of consciousness; from the cessation of consciousness is the cessation of name-and-form; from the cessation of name-and-form is the cessation of the six sense realms; from the cessation of the six sense realms is the cessation of contact ... Thus there is the cessation of this whole mass of suffering.[13]

The six sense realms, contact, feeling, and craving

The first four *nidānas* establish the basic samsaric situation we are in: we find ourselves in the midst of an existence that is imperfect and unsatisfying, in which we experience varying degrees of unsatisfactoriness because of basic ignorance and because of the momentum of our various personality traits and habits. Thinking that we are really our consciousness follows from ignorance; and so does thinking that we are just our physical bodies. The next few *nidānas* go on to describe the perceptual processes whereby the reactive mind operates in ordinary experience.

The experience of the **'six sense realms'** (in Pali, *saḷāyatanāni*, in Sanskrit *ṣaḍāyatanāni*) depends on body and mind together with consciousness. Do we experience anything except via the six senses – what is seen, what is heard, what is smelled, what is tasted, what is touched, and what is thought? Can we know about or feel anything without having first perceived it? This *nidāna* directs our attention to the sixfold gateway via which all our experience happens. It might seem strange to think of the mind as a sense. However, the point is that it is possible to become aware of what is going on in the mind – our thoughts, memories, dreams, fantasies, and so on – without being caught up in it. Through this kind of mindfulness practice we can become aware that there is a difference between the mind as an organ (which thinks) and the *contents* of the mind (thoughts and so on). How much of our *dukkha* and confusion comes from taking too literally what is going on in our minds? Just as we might mistake a rope for a snake in the dark, we can mistake our mental desires and fears for realities about the world, and be unable to gain a more objective perspective.

Dependent on the six sense realms arises **'contact'** (in Pali, *phassa*, in Sanskrit, *sparśa*). Contact refers to the experience of a particular object, whether it is a person seen or heard, some food smelled or tasted, an itch that is felt on the body, or a memory coming into one's mind. The point of identifying this *nidāna* specifically is to highlight how our perceptual experience is not passive. Perceptual experience does not just happen; whether we are aware of it or not, our minds are continuously directing attention to certain objects that occur in the realms of the senses – a sexy person, a scary sound, a cheery thought. Contact is the moment when the object, the sense organ and sense-consciousness come together – our experience is to some degree created out of our active participation in the process of perception.

On condition of contact arises **'feeling'** (in Pali and Sanskrit, *vedanā*). Any particular experience is accompanied by a feeling-tone, which is pleasant, painful, or neutral. Feeling, in this Buddhist sense, does not mean the emotion we feel towards something experienced, but the more immediate felt sense of 'I like it', 'I don't like it', or 'I don't really mind' in relation to what is contacted via eye, ear, nose, tongue, body, or mind. We should not be misled by the presentation in the words of the twelve *nidānas*; in this case, feeling does not arise after contact, but along with it – it co-arises. We do not first contact the taste of a piece of chocolate and then start to enjoy it; the sense-contact and the enjoyment happen together. However, these two *nidānas*, contact and feeling, are distinguished because they relate to different aspects – the receptive and the responsive – of experience. While we can to some extent choose *what* we contact, *what it is like* to contact this object – whether it is enjoyable, disagreeable, or neither – is purely a response.

On condition of feeling arises **'craving'** (in Pali, *taṇhā*, in Sanskrit, *tṛṣṇā*), which we encountered in Chapter Two. Although craving suggests desire, this *nidāna* also includes aversion (as the opposite of longing), which we tend to experience as the secondary emotional reaction to unpleasant feeling. Craving therefore means the experience of 'I want', 'I don't want', or 'I don't really care'. There is another common definition of craving: as craving for sense-pleasures, craving for existence (*bhava*), and craving for non-existence (*vibhava*). This definition widens our sense of what craving implies – not just sensual desire but the longing to be someone, to have a stronger, clearer, better-known self; or the longing to disappear, not to be noticed as a distinct person at all. All this is what we do with feeling. If we are not aware, if we do not deliberately pay attention to the way craving arises on condition of feeling, then we slide from enjoyment to craving and from displeasure to aversion without even noticing it. It is what happens *between* these two *nidānas* that is the primary source of *dukkha*.

The links from the six sense realms to craving are matters that we can become aware of in the present moment, using the *nidānas* to identify different stages in how experience comes about. When we do this we begin to notice something important: between feeling and craving is a 'gap' – a crack in the necessity by which experience unfolds. Whereas feeling *always* arises along with contact, the arising of craving on condition of feeling is *not* a matter of complete necessity; it is possible, if very difficult, to observe feelings without reacting to them. Here is the secret of true contentment, the hidden doorway by which we can escape the rolling wheel – awareness at the junction of feeling and craving. Sangharakshita describes the situation like this:

> The transition from sensation to craving, from passive feeling to active desire, is the psychological fact standing

> behind all myths of the Fall of Man from paradise to earth, from a blissful to a miserable state and sphere of existence. The interval between these two *nidānas* is the battlefield of the spiritual life and to experience feelings yet check desires is that victory over oneself which the Buddha declared to be greater than the conquest of a thousand men a thousand times.[14]

To practise awareness is to bring attention to feeling such that we are less at the mercy of our compulsions. With the spaciousness gained, there is room to manoeuvre.

However, this is not to say that there is anything wrong with feeling. The experience of liking, not liking, or neither, just arises. There is no need to judge feelings; if we did, it would result in a form of craving or aversion added to what is felt. Awareness of feelings is, in itself, enough to create the distance needed for making creative decisions. During the mindfulness of breathing meditation, for instance, we do not attempt to control the breath; we simply become aware of the breathing process, even if it is ragged and shallow. The very awareness tends to have a calming effect. In the same way, when becoming aware of feeling, we attend to the feeling-tone of experience, and notice what it is like. In this way, how we respond to this feeling becomes a more creative and informed choice, rather than a reactive one based in greed, hate, and delusion. This is important because we will no doubt discover that we feel all sorts of things, pleasant and unpleasant, including feelings that we cannot even put into words. These may be the results of our state of bodily health, past conditioning, or even the consequence of past actions. Whatever the source of our feelings, the task of mindfulness is to remain grounded and aware.

As well as applying awareness to the way craving arises in dependence on feeling, we can also apply intelligence to the way contact arises in dependence on the six sense realms. If we have noticed that we are particularly prone, for instance, to guzzle chocolate cake as soon as we've tasted it, making ourselves unwell, then we might benefit from not coming into contact with chocolate cake at all. Similarly, if the sight of a certain person always throws us into a storm of anger and frustration, it may be as well to avoid them until we are better equipped to deal with our reactions, for instance through gaining some insight into the reasons for our reactivity. The process of bringing intelligence to how contact arises dependent on the six sense realms is traditionally called 'guarding the gates of the senses'.[15] The senses are like doors, and we know some experiences cause trouble if we let them in. To guard the senses is sometimes a form of kindness, as it is so easy to overstimulate ourselves thinking that it will give us a boost, when in fact it may just make us feel wrecked.

Clinging, existence, birth, and ageing-and-death

The final *nidānas* give us the Buddha's explanation of rebirth, of how human life will continue its unsatisfactory round in the future. The '**clinging**' or '**grasping**' (in Pali and Sanskrit, *upādāna*) that arises dependent on craving is defined as fourfold: there is grasping at sensual pleasure, clinging to views, clinging to conduct and vows (our beliefs and commitments considered as ends in themselves), and clinging to doctrines and ideas about a permanent Self (ideas about who we really are). Clinging is like the fuel upon which the fires of our greed, aversion, and delusion feed (the word *upādāna* means 'fuel' as well as 'clinging'). This *nidāna* represents the psychological tendency to meld our preferences into an organized sense of who we are, what we believe and what we think the world should be like. There is less good in this than we might like to think. We all know what it is like to meet people who have become fixed and inflexible in their ways. Many of us might have experienced the inside version of this state: a rigidity in ourselves and in our world that feels like prison walls of emotions and views.

Dependent on clinging arises **'existence'** or **'becoming'** (in Pali and Sanskrit, *bhava*). The translation of *bhava* as 'becoming' is useful in this regard, as it has a more dynamic flavour than 'existence', and hence suggests the continuity-within-change that characterizes the Buddha's approach to rebirth. This process of continual becoming is not preordained and inevitable, however; it depends upon the active clinging to pleasures, views, ways of life, and a sense of self. In the more cosmic world view of traditional Buddhism, existence manifests in the various realms of the Wheel of Life. However, we can also think of existence in *this* life: on condition of clinging arises a fixed sense of who we are that can get quite reliable. We wake up knowing who we are, what we like for breakfast, and where we go for our summer holidays. While it all lasts, we usually don't notice that all this – which seems real and dependable at the time – must inevitably change.

'Birth' (in Pali and Sanskrit, *jāti*) depends on existence. Birth traditionally means being born into one or other group of beings (one of the six realms in the Wheel of Life), coming into a womb, and obtaining the senses necessary for more experience. We can, however, also consider birth in a metaphorical sense as relating to the birth of an experience in which, for a while, we are absorbed, and which, while it lasts, we take for granted as being the way it is. This might be a relationship, a marriage, a job, a phase of life, or even a Buddhist retreat. Taking birth metaphorically as birth into some such experience, we know who we are for a while: but everything that is born must die.

Finally, dependent on birth is **'ageing and death'** (in Pali and Sanskrit, *jarā-maraṇa*). Ageing means of course decaying teeth, greying hair, wrinkling skin, and fading senses; death means laying down this body, passing away, leaving behind what you know. Just as birth can be interpreted in a metaphorical as well as a literal sense, so 'ageing and death' can be taken to refer to the fading and passing of experiences in the course of one's life.

'Thus has arisen this whole mass of *dukkha*.' The teaching of the twelve *nidānas* shows in detail the ways in which *dukkha* arises in experience. Happily, the Buddha also taught a way by which it can all be brought to an end.

Questions for Chapter Three

1. What is your response to the three-life interpretation of the twelve *nidānas*? In what ways do you think it might be helpful for modern westerners?
2. Describe some specific examples of how ignorance can give rise to formations. For example, a belief that you always like chocolate might lead you to habitually eat it, even when you don't really want it.
3. Are there any ways in which you already limit contact in order to guard the gates of the senses? Are there any further ways in which it might be useful to do so?
4. Spend five minutes looking for pleasant feeling in your experience, five minutes looking for unpleasant feeling, and five minutes looking for neutral feeling. Which of these is easiest to find? Which is hardest?
5. Reflect on some way in which your sense of identity has changed in your life. What conditions contributed towards this change?
6. How would you like to change your sense of identity in the future? How might you go about it?

Chapter Four

The Spiral Path

In Chapter Three we explored the Buddha's detailed model of twelve *nidānas* through which *dukkha* arises. We might recall that the Buddha also taught that with the cessation of these same *nidānas, dukkha* ceases. That is to say, with the cessation of ignorance, formations cease; with the cessation of formations, consciousness ceases (in the sense of ceasing to be a problem); and so on. And the complete cessation of all these conditions for *dukkha* is synonymous with the attaining of awakening, *bodhi*. It has to be said, though, that this way of talking about the spiritual path as a process of cessation makes Buddhism seem to be a merely negative business of getting rid of what causes pain. This is partly a problem of presentation. The ceasing of the twelve *nidānas* means the systematic undermining and removal of the reactive mode, and this also leaves the creative mind free to illuminate the world with its radiant vitality; which is an entirely positive outcome. In fact the Buddha also taught the way to awakening in positive terms – as a path, or way, consisting of a progressive, dependently arisen series of spiritual experiences of increasing sublimity and creativity.[1]

The factors of the 'spiral path'

The Buddha described the ancient way to awakening in several different ways, using sets of factors linked to one another in various ways. Best known, perhaps, is the eightfold path, in which each of the eight factors is to be cultivated, not one after another, but all at the same time. That is, the eight factors of the eightfold path are not a progressive series so much as a complementary set, like the petals of a flower, which develop together into the full flowering of awakening. Another formulation of the stages of the path is that of ethics (*sīla*), meditation (*samādhi*), and wisdom (*paññā*). Each of these stages is necessary for awakening, but they are also arranged in order: on the basis of a well-established ethical practice it becomes possible to meditate effectively, and on the basis of an effective meditation practice it becomes possible to reflect on the truths of the Dharma and to develop wisdom and insight.[2]

A few Pali discourses, however, preserve a way in which the Buddha taught his path to awakening as a dependently arising series of positive *nidānas*.[3] One discourse, the Upanisā Sutta, attaches these positive factors to the twelve *nidānas* of conditioned existence in what appears to be a positive counterpart to the *nidānas* that give rise to *dukkha*.[4] The resulting series describes the whole scope of human experience, from ignorance to awakening, all of it arising according to the teaching of conditionality. In the following extract the Buddha gives his monks a summary of this integrated account of the whole of conditionality:

> So, Bhikkhus, ignorance is the basis (*upanisā*) for formations, formations are the basis for consciousness, consciousness is the basis for name-and-form, name-and-form is the basis for the six sense realms, the six sense realms are the basis for contact, contact is the basis for feeling, feeling is the basis for craving, craving is the basis for clinging, clinging is the basis for existence, existence is the basis for birth, birth is the basis for *dukkha*, *dukkha* is the basis for faith, faith is the basis for joy, joy is the basis for rapture, rapture is the basis for tranquillity, tranquillity is the basis for bliss, bliss is the basis for concentration, concentration is the basis for knowledge and vision of reality, knowledge and vision of reality is the basis for disenchantment, disenchantment is the basis for dispassion, dispassion is the basis for liberation, and liberation is the basis for knowledge about destruction.[5]

In this series the Buddha teaches the twelve *nidānas* of samsara as culminating not with ageing and death, but simply with *dukkha*. This substitution draws our attention to the function of the twelve *nidānas* as a whole of explaining the complex arising of unsatisfactoriness, and not only of rebirth.

Dukkha and faith are given as the beginning stages of the spiritual journey. With awareness of the unsatisfactoriness of existence, and with faith in the Dharma, we set out: we go for refuge to the three jewels, we meditate, and perhaps we go on retreat. Other discourses, as we shall see, also describe ethical practice and wise attention as initial conditions for the path. On condition of having discovered and begun practising the Buddha's way to awakening arises the joy of having found a path, and on that basis arise a series of factors concerned with psychic integration and maturation: rapture, tranquillity, bliss, and concentration. Meditative concentration is then the basis for knowledge and vision of reality, which is direct total insight into the human condition. On this basis arise some final factors concerned with liberation – disenchantment, dispassion, liberation, and knowledge about destruction (of *dukkha*) – which are more or less synonymous, being different aspects of the awakening experience. In other discourses 'knowledge about destruction' is replaced with 'knowledge and vision of liberation'; this factor is synonymous with the realization of nirvana.

Whereas the conditions described by the twelve links of samsara merely reinforce the tendency of the reactive mind to revolve and remain stuck, the factors of the path consist of expansion, opening, unravelling, enlargement, and ascent. Therefore, whereas the conditionality of the twelve links can be described in terms of the turning of a wheel, the conditionality that describes the creative mind can be represented in the form of a spiral, and has been described by Sangharakshita like this:

> The nature of spiritual development is perhaps most clearly seen in terms of the spiral mode of conditionality, in which it is represented as a certain sequence of experiences, one experience arising in dependence upon

> another. Just as out of the bud grows the flower, and out of the flower the fruit, so out of one spiritual experience there grows another, out of that yet another, and out of that another still, each one higher, more refined, more beautiful, a little nearer to nirvana. Each stage is a spiritual experience in the process of transition to another, more advanced experience. The stages aren't fixed or static; you don't proceed up the spiral path like going up the steps of a staircase, even a spiral staircase. We speak of 'the Buddhist path' or 'the spiritual path', but we mustn't be misled by the metaphor. It isn't that the spiritual path is fixed and rigid, and we just go up it; or that we move but the path remains stationary. The path itself grows, just like a plant grows, one stage passing over into the next so that there's a constant upward movement.[6]

The 'spiral path' can be represented as emerging from the 'gap' between feeling and craving, that is, from an awareness of existence as unsatisfactory. It leads away from the mechanical repetitions of the reactive mind, and outwards through a series of dependently arisen experiences, each more refined than the last. With 'knowledge and vision of reality' arises liberating insight. But even this step is not the end. Nirvana, the culmination of the path, is not so much the end of the journey as complete freedom from limitation.[7]

Opening stages of the path

According to the Upanisā Sutta, faith arises on condition of *dukkha*; however, we cannot take this too literally. Clearly *dukkha* alone is not sufficient to bring about faith, or else the whole of humanity would be following a spiritual path. The point, perhaps, is that *dukkha* is a condition in the sense of a spur to re-evaluating things; it reveals the basic insecurity of the human condition. Our response to basic *dukkha*, unpleasant feeling, is generally aversion, avoidance and escape. But when we bring awareness

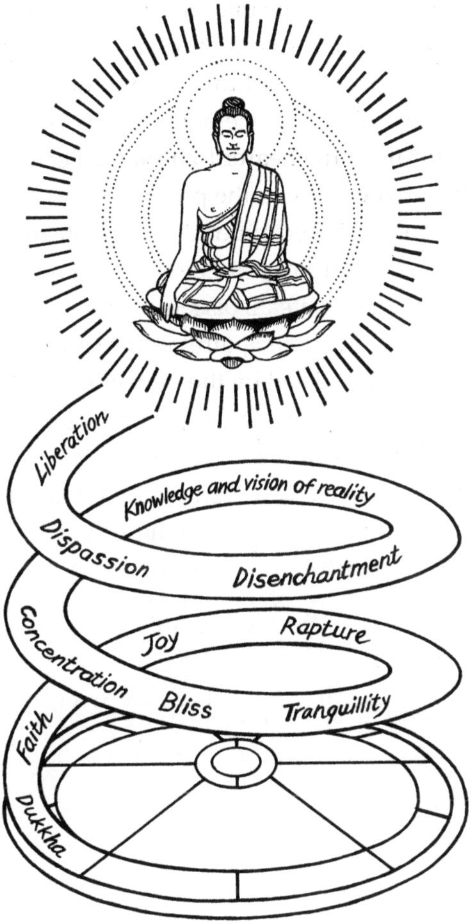

Figure 3: *The 'Spiral Path': twelve progressive factors of the path arising from the twelve nidānas of samsara. (© Saddharāja.)*

to this experience of *dukkha* we begin to open up a gap in which we can make more reflective and creative choices about how we act on feeling. We might realize that the causes of unhappiness lie as much in ourselves as in the outside world. Our awareness of *dukkha* creates room for faith in the possibility of a path towards freedom.

The path from *dukkha* to faith manifests in different ways. It may be a sense of unsatisfactoriness with the material things in life and a desire to find greater meaning; or we may be prompted by an accident or serious illness with a desire to live more fully while there is still the chance; or the death of someone we love may lead us to search for something to fill the gap in our lives. In all cases there is a restlessness that comes from realizing that life is not entirely satisfactory and wishing to search for something better. If we succeed in hearing the Dharma at this point, then the conditions are present for faith in the three jewels to arise.

'Faith' (*saddhā* in Pali, *śraddhā* in Sanskrit) in Buddhism means confidence and trust – it does not mean blind belief. Sangharakshita writes that 'faith consists in deep conviction of what is real, lucidity as to what has value, and longing for what is possible.'[8] It means faith in the three jewels of Buddhism: the

technical terms in Buddhism

saddhā

(in Pali; in Sanskrit, *śraddhā*), means 'placing' (*dhā*) ourselves in or on the 'truth' (*śrad*). The word *śrad* comes from an old Indo-European word that appears in Latin as *cor*, in Greek as *kardia*, and in English as 'heart', so in a poetic sense we can say that *śraddhā* means 'placing the heart'. Sangharakshita describes faith as 'the response of what is ultimate in us to what is ultimate in the universe'. The Pali discourses describe the person of faith as one who puts their trust in the awakening of the Buddha thus: 'The Blessed One is an *arahant*, completely awakened, consummate in knowledge and practice, the joyful one, yet worldly wise, unsurpassed trainer of persons to be tamed, the teacher of devas and human beings, the Buddha, the Blessed One.'

Buddha, the Dharma and the Sangha; confidence that the Buddha was awakened, that the Dharma corresponds to the way things really are, and that the Sangha (the Buddhist spiritual community) contains individuals who to some extent practise the Buddha's teaching. Faith can be thought of as the capacity to respond to what is truly of value. It can manifest as a delight in beauty, as rejoicing in virtue (both in others and in ourselves), as a desire for the truth, as a respect for spiritual values, and as devotion towards images and symbols that embody those ideals. Such a faith does not involve belief in God or supernatural agency, but is an intuition about the possibility of spiritual evolution inherent in the nature of things. The English poet William Wordsworth evokes such a faith in these lines from his poem 'Tintern Abbey':

And I have felt
A presence that disturbs me with the joy
Of elevated thoughts; a sense sublime
Of something far more deeply interfused,
Whose dwelling is the light of setting suns,
And the round ocean and the living air,
And the blue sky, and in the mind of man;
A motion and a spirit, that impels
All thinking things, all objects of all thought,
And rolls through all things.[9]

We may be used to the idea of faith as emotional assent, manifest in the way people give themselves over to what they believe in. For Buddhists, however, *saddhā* has broader connotations. It has three aspects: a cognitive or intellectual aspect, an emotional aspect, and a volitional aspect. *Cognitive* or *intellectual faith* means being convinced by the Dharma. It comes by thinking things through; for instance, by reading a Dharma book, and by reflecting on or discussing it. We might experience *emotional faith* when we are moved by and drawn to positive qualities in someone we see living the Buddhist life, or perhaps through doing *pūjā* or some other act of devotion. We might also experience a heartfelt faith when we long to change or when we have a quiet confidence in the path we are following. *Volitional faith* means being convinced enough to act on our ideals and having faith in our capacity to practise the Dharma; it means speaking up for one's ethical values as well as meditating every morning no matter how we are feeling.

How does faith develop? It is not necessarily something mysterious, and certainly not a matter of grace. Sangharakshita describes faith as grounded in intuition, reason, and experience.[10] Faith in the three jewels might start as a matter of *intuition*, that is, as a hunch that meditation or Buddhism has something to offer us. Faith builds up from there through our experience that the Dharma works. Our first attraction to the Dharma is often intuitive. We hear or see something that resonates with us, and this motivates us to explore further. We might enthusiastically throw ourselves into discovering more. But sooner or later we start to question the teachings we have heard; we want to clarify what is meant and to weigh what others tell us against our own ideas and experience. We may become critical. If we can keep questioning in order to discover the truth for ourselves, while maintaining momentum in our practice, we are developing faith grounded in *reason*. Eventually we develop some experience of the truth of the Dharma. We have a lived understanding that does not depend on borrowed concepts. This is faith grounded in *experience*.

Once we have experienced some faith in the Buddhist path, we may begin to experience the joy of knowing we are on the right track in life. According to the Upanisā Sutta this joy develops out of faith; however, the Upanisā Sutta is just one of the Pali discourses that describe progressive stages of the path.[11] In several other suttas the stage of joy is described as supported not by faith, but by ethics.[12] In these suttas, being established in virtue and ethical conduct leads to freedom from remorse, and freedom from remorse leads to joy. Buddhist ethics (*sīla*, or in Sanskrit, *śīla*) are summarized in the five training precepts undertaken by all Buddhists, namely, refraining from harming living beings, stealing, sexual misconduct, lying, and intoxication.

There is a close connection between faith and keeping the Buddhist ethical precepts. The traditional way in which Buddhists express their faith is by declaring that they go for refuge to the three jewels; and they then undertake to keep the five training precepts as a practical expression of their going for refuge. If we recognize the Buddha as our teacher, and the Dharma as the way to awakening, then it follows that we will want to live our lives with the dignity of knowing that we hold to standards of behaviour that benefit ourselves and those around us, standards exemplified by the Buddha and his awakened followers. When we are established in ethical conduct, what follows is freedom from remorse (*avippaṭisāra*).

The experience of freedom from remorse can be compared to looking up and down the path of one's life and finding it open and uncluttered by regret; your conscience is clear, and you see nothing for which you need to make amends. Of course, this does not happen by magic. Once you begin to establish yourself in ethics by practising the precepts, you begin to learn how to sort out your mistakes and regrets. First, we allow ourselves to feel shame about our unwholesome actions.[13] Then, confessing our mistakes to spiritual friends becomes possible, allowing us to air our shame and receive help and support.[14] Out of shame comes the resolve not to let ourselves down again. It may be that we can make amends in some way for what we have done; or, if this is not possible, our inner remorse and resolve allow us to be sorry and to let go. In this way, freedom from remorse arises, and from this experience comes an inner lightness and joy.

Another sutta describes this joy as arising from 'wise attention' (*yoniso manasikāra*).[15] *Manasikāra* literally means 'doing in the mind', and what we do in our minds can be thoughtful and ethical, or not. The word *yoniso* means 'according to the origin' (a *yoni* is a womb, a creative source), so *yoniso manasikāra* is the kind of attention that looks for the basic truths of things. It is a quality of reflective thoughtfulness that is not content just to go along with conventional ideas, but wants to peel back surface appearances to get to what is really there.[16] Wise attention is a forerunner of wisdom, the beginning of the path to insight. We might reflect on how everything changes, and how interconnected our lives are; such reflection works against self-centredness. We might reflect on how even people we don't like have some good qualities; this keeps us open to them as human beings. Wise attention thus connects with ethics and faith. We can cultivate wise attention in many smaller ways too; for instance, before we eat a meal we might pause and consider the many people involved in the cultivation and preparation of our food. Such a consideration brings us into a more direct relationship with how we human beings depend on one another.

The path from joy to insight

We have seen, then, that there are three different conditions given in the early Buddhist discourses for the arising of joy on the spiritual path:

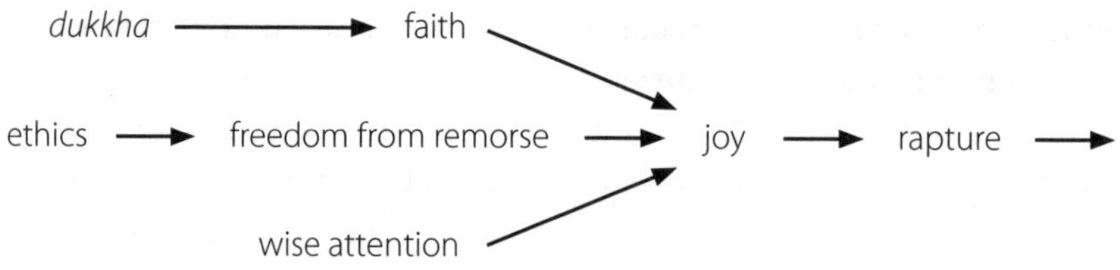

'Joy' (*pāmojja*, in Sanskrit *prāmodya*) means gladness and delight. The meaning of this stage is that we experience an emotional sense of having found a path or way; through faith, through ethics, or through our thinking, we have arrived at a certain clarity of direction in life. When you have had a glimpse of what you are looking for, there is a lifting of the heart and a natural joy. You have an aim in life, and that by itself brings some satisfaction. This joy confirms confidence in the teaching and so strengthens faith, so that faith and joy are mutually reinforcing. Of course, it is not necessarily as straightforward as this. We may have found the Dharma and yet not feel much joy, for other reasons. However, it is important to look for joy in our experience and to relish it when it is present, as it sets the emotional tone for the following stages of the path, which involve increasing positivity.

In dependence upon joy arises rapture (in Pali *pīti*, in Sanskrit, *prīti)*; an intense, thrilling, ecstatic rapture that pervades the body from head to foot. You might have had some experience of such rapture while listening to music, in the beauty of nature, or in deep and warm communication with a close friend. In the Buddhist context it is most often experienced during meditation, though it is not limited to it. Rapture has several levels, from pleasure to transporting ecstasy: the first level consists merely in the raising of the hairs on the body; then comes rapture like flashes of lightning; then there is the rapture that breaks over the body in waves; at the fourth level the body is said to levitate (perhaps this is how it feels); and finally rapture is said to pervade the whole body like water filling a cave.[17] The experience of this much physical bliss can have a huge effect on the way we think and feel about life, for it is a kind of pleasure that is completely wholesome, healthy, and free. In meditation it is entirely internal, and it proves that great pleasure can be found in the simple act of sitting and calming the mind. Sangharakshita explains the place of rapture in the process of psychological integration:

> To use modern terminology, one could say that rapture comes about as a result of the release of blocked energy – energy that is short-circuiting itself, as it were, or as if locked up. In the course of one's spiritual life, especially when one practises meditation, these blocks get dissolved. One digs down, one uncovers certain depths within oneself; little complexes are resolved, so that energy locked up in them is released and surges up. It's due to this upsurge of energy, felt throughout the nervous system as well as the mind, that one experiences *prīti*.[18]

We could say that at this stage the spiritual path itself becomes thrilling and rapturous, as old habits are undone and blocked energies are released.

In dependence upon rapture arises tranquillity (*passaddhi*, in Sanskrit *praśrabdhi*). The relatively rough, physical quality of rapture calms down, and what is left is a calmer sense of bodily serenity. This stage arises quite organically as we become sated with rapture; its thrill begins to feel a bit too bright, and we are ready for what Sangharakshita describes as the 'integrated exhilaration' of *passaddhi*.[19] Even this exhilaration eventually subsides, however, and what is then left is an intense non-sensual mental bliss (*sukha*). This is a form of deep inner happiness and contentment that emerges in meditation as inner tensions dissolve; it is the intense sense of well-being that is left as one abandons the five hindrances of sensual desire, ill will, sloth and torpor, restlessness and anxiety, and doubt.

The happy mind is capable of intense concentration (*samādhi*). The word *samādhi* means a 'coming together of thought', which signifies something more than mental focus. When our minds have become purified through rapture, have calmed down, and are resting in deep well-being, our mental and emotional energies can flow undistractedly into whatever we are doing. This integrated flow is *samādhi*, and such concentration itself supports ongoing happiness. The Buddha was capable of long periods of uninterrupted blissful concentration, and he taught the importance of the experience of such bliss to counter the idea that spiritual life is only about bearing with suffering. In the following exchange he is talking to followers of Nigaṇṭha Nāṭaputta, the leader of the Jains, who believed that suffering was the way to purify past bad karma:

> 'What do you think, Nigaṇṭhas – can King Seniya Bimbisāra of Māgadha live experiencing absolute bliss without moving his body and without speaking a word for seven days and nights ... six days and nights ... or even for one day and night?'
>
> 'No, friend, he cannot.'
>
> 'But, Nigaṇṭhas, I can live experiencing absolute bliss without moving my body and without speaking a word not just for one day and night ... for two days and nights ... but for seven days and nights. This being the case, what do you think, Nigaṇṭhas – who lives in the greater bliss, King Seniya Bimbisāra of Magadha or me?'
>
> 'This being the case, the Venerable Gotama lives in greater bliss than King Seniya Bimbisāra of Magadha.'[20]

The comparison of the Buddha's bliss to that of King Bimbisāra relies on the idea that the King, who with all his power and wealth can do as he pleases, ought to be the happier. But it is not so, because the Buddha's bliss is internal and non-sensual, and continually refreshed through concentration.

For those of us who have not yet experienced the bliss of a Buddha, the message of these teachings on the stages of the path is that concentration will come as we become happier and more content, and that this happiness is itself based on developing faith, ethics, and wise attention. The seeds from which grows a contented and concentrated mind are simple acts like doing a kind deed, reading an inspiring text, or paying attention to what we appreciate in ourselves or in our friends.

Deep concentration is not, however, the end of the Buddhist path. Even if we attain to highly concentrated states, we may later find ourselves reactive and falling into old habits. It is only by eradicating the deep-seated tendencies to act from ignorance and craving that it is possible to obtain lasting liberation. Craving, and the ignorance upon which it arises, are eliminated by insight – direct knowing and seeing in personal experience of how things come to be, and how they pass away again. This is not just intellectual understanding. Primarily it comes from clear and undistracted awareness, which arises dependent on concentration.

This is the stage of knowledge and vision of reality (*yathā-bhūta-ñāṇa-dassana*). By 'reality' here I do not mean that there is something 'real' apart from this conditioned existence, only that we experience conditioned existence as it really is. The term 'insight' (*vipassanā*) denotes the breakthrough to this experience. The teaching of the 'three characteristics of conditioned existence' (the three *lakkhaṇas*, or, in Sanskrit, the *lakṣaṇas*) gives us a taste of what it is we might directly know and see through insight: all conditioned things are impermanent (*anicca*), unsatisfactory (*dukkha*), and insubstantial (*anatta*). These characteristics, to be explored further in Chapter Seven, follow from the truth of conditionality. Because everything is conditioned, it is always in a state of flux, and changes as conditions change. Our bodies, our feelings, our thoughts – everything we experience is impermanent and changing. Change means that there is nothing that could provide us with lasting and certain happiness, and hence conditioned things are intrinsically incapable of satisfying us. Finally, if things are constantly changing and ultimately unsatisfactory they are insubstantial, without a permanent reliable essence or Self.

If you have penetrated to these truths with your whole being, your life will never be the same. The vision of existence experienced at this stage in the path is traditionally associated with 'stream entry', meaning entry into the stream that leads ineluctably to complete awakening; it is an irreversible vision of reality. A characteristic of a stream entrant is that they have unwavering faith in the Buddha, Dharma and Sangha.[21] So the spiritual path that began with faith has reached a certain culmination.

Insight, liberation, and awakening

For most of us, the stages of the path that arise dependent on insight will seem rather remote. Nevertheless, it might be useful to know what to expect as we travel along the Buddhist path. The stages of the path marked by disenchantment (*nibbidā*) and dispassion (*virāga*) are often put together; they are not really separate stages so much as further consequences of insight. When we realize how things are not dependable because they are constantly changing, we no longer seek after them. There is no longer any wish for gratification of desires, as they are seen not to lead to any lasting satisfaction. This is disenchantment. You may already have some experience of this at some level; for example, when you were younger you may have collected dolls or cars, but at a certain age you could no longer see the point. While disenchantment marks the movement away from involvement in what used to fascinate or disturb us, dispassion is the state of being detached. It is an attitude of relinquishment and consequently of imperturbability. It is certainly not incompatible with compassion for beings, but you keep a broad perspective. You no longer get caught up emotionally in what you know will change.

Disenchantment and dispassion are stages of the path very close to awakening; in a way, they are different aspects of the awakening experience. The next stage, liberation (*vimutti*, in Sanskrit, *vimukti*), means release or complete spiritual freedom. The heart and mind that is liberated is free from ignorance, craving, and clinging; it is free from the reactive mode of operation. It is also free to operate entirely in the creative mode – and free for all-pervading *mettā* or loving-kindness.

Beyond the stage of liberation is the stage of knowing that one is liberated, and that the pollutants (*āsavas*) are destroyed. These pollutants are a Buddhist way of indicating the most fundamental sources of greed, hate, and delusion in experience. There is the pollutant of desire for sensual pleasure; the pollutant of craving for any form of existence; and the pollutant that consists in spiritual ignorance. With the destruction of these pollutants and the clear knowledge that they are destroyed comes the end of the path. This culmination is expressed in a passage common in the Pali discourses as a description of awakening:

> One understands as it really is: 'This is *dukkha*, this is the origin of *dukkha*, this is the cessation of *dukkha*, this is the path to the cessation of *dukkha*. These are the pollutants, this is the origin of the pollutants, this is the cessation of the pollutants. This is the path to the cessation of the pollutants.' As one is knowing and seeing thus, one's mind is liberated from the pollutant of sensuality, from the pollutant of existence, and from the pollutant of ignorance. When one is liberated, the knowledge arises in one: 'I have been liberated'; and one understands that birth is destroyed, the holy life has been lived, what was to be done has been done, and there is no further existence like this.[22]

We see in this description how the culmination of the Buddhist spiritual life is set out entirely in terms of conditionality, so that the *dukkha* that has arisen now ceases with the arising of knowledge of being liberated. But to talk about 'knowledge of liberation' or 'knowledge and vision of destruction' is to attempt to express something nearly inexpressible. How can one put into words the opening out of experience into infinite creativity and freedom? Inevitably, it is easier to talk of what has been destroyed, given up, and left behind. The spiral path leads into inconceivable liberation.

Two images for the path

We have seen that Sangharakshita has described the path to awakening as a spiral, suggesting an opening and expanding in contrast to the closed cycle of the *nidānas* of samsara. We also find two other (and complementary) images for the path in the Pali discourses. The first is an image of water flowing down a mountain, pouring and overflowing, following its course to the sea – a common image for attaining nirvana:

> Just as, monks, when it rains huge drops on the tops of mountains, the water pouring down the slopes fills up (*paripūreti*) the branching clefts of mountain gullies; the full up branching clefts of mountain gullies fill up ponds; the full up ponds fill up lakes; the full up lakes fill up streams; the full up streams fill up rivers; and the full up rivers fill up the great ocean. Likewise, monks, ignorance is the basis (*upanisā*) for formations, formations are the basis for consciousness, consciousness is the basis for name-and-form, name-and-form is the basis for the six sense realms, the six sense realms are the basis for contact, contact is the basis for feeling, feeling is the basis for craving, craving is the basis for clinging, clinging is the basis for existence, existence is the basis for birth, birth is the basis for pain, pain is the basis for faith, faith is the basis for joy, joy is the basis for rapture, rapture is the basis for tranquillity, tranquillity is the basis for bliss, bliss is the basis for concentration, concentration is the basis for knowledge and vision of reality, knowledge and vision of reality is the basis for disenchantment, disenchantment is the basis for dispassion, dispassion is the basis for liberation, and liberation is the basis for knowledge about destruction.[23]

The second image, of a tree coming into full maturity, similarly follows and illustrates an account of factors of the path, this time beginning with ethics and freedom from remorse:

> It's as if, monks, there was a tree flourishing with branches and leaves; its bark-crust will attain to complete development (*pāripūriṃ gacchati*), and its inner bark, sapwood, and heartwood will attain to complete development. In the same way, monks, for someone ethical and established in virtuous conduct, the secret cause (*upanisā*) of freedom from remorse is fulfilled. When there is freedom from remorse, for someone with perfect freedom from remorse, the secret cause of joy is fulfilled [and so on through the factors of the path until] ... the secret cause of knowledge and vision of liberation is fulfilled.[24]

These positive images illustrate the Buddhist path, comparing it to the flowing and gathering of waters, and to the full maturation of some magnificent living tree. English translation cannot, however, easily bring out the wordplay that links these images and connects them to an underlying metaphor of fullness and completion. The word *paripūreti* is used to describe the 'overflowing' of water as it flows from stream to pond to river; and the parts of a tree are said to *paripūriṃ gacchati*, literally 'it goes to fullness', that is, 'attains complete development'. And hence, in another discourse, the Buddha describes the factors of the path (called simply 'states') in terms of overflowing, fulfilment, and completion:

> Thus, monks, states (*dhammā*) as it were overflow into states, states as it were fulfil (*paripūrenti*) states, in order to go from here to the beyond.[25]

The Buddha thus vividly describes the conditionality of the path as progressive, each factor augmenting the previous as it encourages the arising of the next, in a series that opens into the infinity of the creative mind.

How to approach the path

One of the discourses that describe the dependent arising of the path also provides some useful advice on how to approach the treading of this way to awakening. Giving rise to the succeeding factor is not a matter of deliberately trying to bring it into existence, by wilful effort or by making a wish. Instead, the teaching of conditionality encourages us to consider how 'states overflow into states'; how the path unfolds in its own time and through a natural inner process:

> For someone who is ethical, monks, someone established in virtuous conduct, it is not necessary to be wilful, wishing 'may I have freedom from remorse.' It is natural (*dhammatā*), monks, that for someone who is ethical and who is established in virtuous conduct, freedom from remorse arises.
>
> For someone who is free from remorse, monks, it is not necessary to be wilful, wishing 'may I feel joy.' It is natural, monks, that in someone who is free from remorse joy is born.
>
> For someone who is joyful, monks, it is not necessary to be wilful, wishing 'may I feel rapture.' It is natural, monks, that for someone who is joyful rapture arises.
>
> For someone whose mind is rapturous, monks, it is not necessary to be wilful, wishing 'may my body calm down.' It is natural, monks, that for someone whose mind is rapturous their body calms down.
>
> For someone whose body has calmed down, monks, it is not necessary to be wilful, wishing 'may I experience bliss.' It is natural, monks, that for someone whose body has calmed down they experience bliss.
>
> For someone who is blissful, monks, it is not necessary to be wilful, wishing 'may my mind become concentrated.' It is natural, monks, that for someone who is blissful their mind becomes concentrated.

> For someone who is concentrated, monks, it is not necessary to be wilful, wishing 'may I know and see reality.' It is natural, monks, that for someone who is concentrated they know and see reality.
>
> For someone who knows and sees reality, monks, it is not necessary to be wilful, wishing 'may I be disenchanted, may I be dispassionate.' It is natural, monks, that someone knowing and seeing reality is disenchanted and dispassionate.
>
> For someone who has become disenchanted and dispassionate, monks, it is not necessary to be wilful, wishing 'may I realize the knowing and seeing of liberation.' It is natural, monks, that someone who has become disenchanted and dispassionate realizes the knowing and seeing of liberation.[26]

This advice is especially useful for our meditation practice. Some of us may have had the experience of touching on some inner bliss in meditation, and then consciously and perhaps wilfully chasing after it, only for it to disappear, leaving us excited but empty. But 'it is not necessary to be wilful': our task is just to cultivate the conditions upon which rapture arises, that is, faith, ethical practice, and joy. With these conditions in place, it is natural that rapture will arise when our minds and hearts are ready. In one of his homely agricultural comparisons, the Buddha compares this natural arising to the way that chicks will hatch out of their eggs when they are ready; the hen's job is just to incubate them properly. Likewise, as long as we live devoted to spiritual development, progress will inevitably come about.[27]

This advice from the Buddha leads to the down-to-earth conclusion that our job is simply to put ourselves into whatever stage we are at on the spiritual path, and trust that progress will take care of itself. For most of us that means attending carefully to our ethics: keeping the precepts, refining our speech and action, looking for ways to be generous. But, as the Buddha told Ānanda, this stage of the path is the necessary starting point for the stages that follow:

> Ānanda, the point and benefit of virtuous conduct is freedom from remorse; the point and benefit of freedom from remorse is joy; the point and benefit of joy is rapture; the point and benefit of rapture is tranquillity; the point and benefit of tranquillity is bliss; the point and benefit of bliss is concentration; the point and benefit of concentration is knowledge and vision of reality; the point and benefit of knowledge and vision of reality is dispassion and disenchantment; the point and benefit of dispassion and disenchantment is knowledge and vision of liberation. So, Ānanda, good conduct leads gradually to the very highest state.[28]

The teaching of conditionality therefore encourages us to let go of the idea of getting anywhere in our spiritual lives. The spiritual path exists; it leads to awakening, eventually; and it will unfold – our lives will come to complete fulfillment – through a progressive process that takes care of itself. Of course, we need to make an effort to cultivate ethics, meditation, and wisdom. But we cannot force spiritual growth and development; the path unfolds according to the principle of conditionality.

Questions for Chapter Four

1. Draw a diagram of a similar form to the one in Chapter One for stress to show which conditions help you to feel happier and more contented. Which of these conditions are easiest for you to influence?
2. Describe your experience of faith based on thinking, faith based on an emotional response, and volitional faith. Has the balance changed over time for you?
3. What is the difference between faith (in the Buddhist sense) and beliefs?
4. What conditions started you on your spiritual quest? What conditions have been helpful to you as you have gone deeper?
5. In your experience, what are the conditions that aid concentration in meditation?
6. Are there any things that you used to crave but do so no longer as you have realized that they are not worth the effort of striving to obtain them?

Part Two

The Implications of Conditionality

Chapter Five

Karma, Conditionality, and Ethics

We have explored conditionality as the core teaching of the Dharma, and the fundamental expression of the Buddha's insight into reality. Things arise on certain conditions, and cease when those conditions are no longer present. We have also seen how the Buddha's teaching is a practical one, concerned with the conditions under which *dukkha* arises in human experience, and with the conditions that lead to true well-being and awakening. In this chapter we will explore the Buddha's application of the principle of conditionality to ethical life in his teaching about karma, seeing how the ethical quality of the intentions behind our actions is the condition for experiencing their consequences.

The Buddha's teaching on karma

To understand the Buddha's teaching on karma, which is rather subtle, we need to know something of the context in which he taught. In India at the time of the Buddha, many people believed that what happened to them was somehow bound up with their karma.[1] The word literally means 'action', but 'karma' also has the pregnant sense of 'action that creates the future', so that people believed that their lives were the result of past karmas bearing fruit, and that their present karmas would determine their fate. For the brahmans of the Buddha's day, karma was understood in a ritual and religious sense. Brahman priests were supposed to keep various rules of conduct, and good karma kept them in a state of ritual purity, leading to a good rebirth. If they did something wrong, they could take a ritual bath and chant mantras to purify themselves. The Buddha, however, taught that such religious rituals were in reality useless, and that one could only be 'purified' through ethical actions, by living according to ethical precepts.[2]

The Jains, meanwhile, understood karma to be an invisible material substance that clings to the soul (*jīva*).[3] Every karma or action weighs you down more, keeping you trapped in samsara. While bad actions lead to unpleasant rebirths, good actions lead to pleasant; but the point is to free the soul from karma altogether. The Jains taught that liberation came from making as little new karma as possible, and wearing away past karma though self-mortification. The Buddha also gave an ethical (rather than ritualistic) interpretation of karma, but disagreed with the idea that karma is a fixed substance. He thought this was too literal. Instead he developed his own idea of karma, in which pleasant and unpleasant consequences arise as a result of the ethical quality of the intentions behind actions.[4]

The Buddha's teaching on karma as an application of conditionality can be summed up in the wise old saying: 'Sow an act, and you reap a habit. Sow a habit, and you reap a character. Sow a character, and you reap a destiny.' A story in the Pali canon shows how the Buddha explained his idea. Two young men, Vāseṭṭha and Bhāradvāja, were arguing about whether one becomes a brahman (regarded as the best sort of person) by birth (*jāti*) or by ritual conduct (karma). They took their question to the Buddha, who replied that one was a brahman by karma; but he redefined karma as people's daily doings, that is, their 'work'. Social status arises from what people do:

> By action (karma) one becomes a farmer, by action one becomes a craftsman;
> By action one becomes a trader; by action one becomes a servant.
> By action one also becomes a thief; by action one becomes a soldier;

By action one becomes a priest; by action one becomes a King.
Thus the wise who see dependent arising, familiar
With the ripening of karma, see this action as it really is.
The world rolls on because of action; because of action society turns;
Beings are fastened by action like the moving chariot-wheel by a lynchpin.[5]

For the Buddha, social status is not the result of birth or of doing rituals, but depends on your actions. Hence the Buddha's sangha was a meritocracy, and the men and women who joined it gave up their inherited social roles. The monk Upāli, for instance, had been a barber, a lowly profession according to Indian social standards of the time, but in the Buddha's sangha he became the monk most renowned for his mastery of monastic discipline (*vinaya*).

The Buddha therefore taught that karma means 'action' in an ordinary sense. It is because of what you do, day after day, that you become a certain sort of person, not because of your ritual actions, as the brahmans believed. Actions lead to habits lead to character leads to destiny. Much more importantly, however, the Buddha taught that the ethical quality of one's ordinary actions leads to consequences experienced here and now or in future lives as pleasant or unpleasant. In terms of traditional Buddhist cosmology, and as pictured on the Wheel of Life, actions done through states of greed, hate, and delusion lead after death to misery and rebirth in lower realms, whereas actions done through states of contentment, love, and wisdom lead to happiness in heaven. In traditional Buddhist terminology, good actions are called 'skilful' and negative ones 'unskilful'.

Whether or not we take literally the idea that we will be reborn in one of the six realms after our death, the Buddha's teaching on karma is applicable on the psychological level in the here and now. Through our karma we are each responsible for the kind of person we become and the kind of world we live in. The Buddha recommends that everyone reflect in this sobering way:

technical terms in Buddhism

skilful and unskilful

Buddhism very often uses the word 'skilful' (in Pali *kusala*; in Sanskrit *kuśala*) for good, ethically wholesome actions, and 'unskilful' (*akusala/akuśala*) for bad, ethically unwholesome actions. A skilful action is so-called because it arises from an ability to think and feel in an ethical way; skilful actions are also so-called because they conduce to concentration in meditation. Skilful actions arise from positive mental and emotional intentions, whereas unskilful actions come from negative ones. Practising Buddhist ethics means not just keeping the precepts as an external observance but cultivating the positive, wholesome mental states that lead to skilful actions.

> I am the owner of my actions, heir to my actions, born of my actions, joined to my actions, and actions are my refuge. Whatever actions I might do, good (*kalyāṇa*) or bad (*pāpaka*), of these I will be the heir.[6]

As well as describing actions as an inheritance we give to our own future selves, the Buddha describes karmas (intentional actions) and their results using organic similes: karmas are like seeds, which sooner or later ripen and bear fruit. The language suggests a natural process, and amounts to the application of *paṭicca-samuppāda* to morals: skilful actions ripen as pleasant experiences, unskilful actions as unpleasant. Because it is natural, this process of actions 'ripening' is also inevitable; the past will always catch up with you:

> Not in the sky, nor in the midst of the sea, nor by hiding
> in a mountain cave:
> No place on earth is to be found where one might escape
> one's wicked deeds.[7]

Through their actions, human beings create their destinies. A life devoted to acts of care and generosity will inevitably have consequences experienced as pleasant, whereas selfish acts give rise to unpleasantness, though these results may not be apparent in this life.

We sometimes hear about the 'law of karma', and about how karma means that everyone gets what they deserve, either in this life, or in future lifetimes. In practice, however, the Buddha said that trying to work out the results of karma could drive you crazy.[8] The various stories in the Buddhist scriptures about karma and its consequences, such as rebirth in heaven or hell, are part of a system of religious beliefs that cannot be explained or proved; they are an imaginative system of ethical correspondences. This approach seems to go back to the Buddha. In one discourse the Buddha lists some definite equations between certain actions and their consequences, such that, for instance, not killing leads to long life in subsequent lifetimes, while killing leads to being short-lived.[9] However, in another more philosophical discourse he explains with great subtlety how it is impossible to be sure what will happen to anyone in future lives: for instance, a murderer may be reborn in heaven because of many good deeds done in yet earlier lives.[10] We should therefore understand the Buddha's teaching on karma as a general principle based on conditionality, the point of which is to encourage us to behave ethically.

Before we go on to study the details of the Buddha's teaching about karma, we need to clear up two possible misunderstandings. The Buddha did not teach that everything that happens to us is a result of past karma. The literalistic Jains, however, did believe this. Jain religious practice included bearing with painful experience in order to purify past karma. A wanderer named Sīvaka once asked the Buddha whether this Jain view was correct, and the Buddha told him:

> Saying 'whatever a person experiences, pleasant, unpleasant or neither, all this is caused by what was done in the past,' they exceed what is known by oneself, they exceed what is considered true in the world; therefore I say that those ascetics and brahmans are wrong.[11]

The Buddha was being practical. Saying that everything we experience is as a result of past actions is just a belief, beyond what anyone can know personally or even what is generally believed. But the Buddha taught that experience arises on conditions; and he goes on to tell Sīvaka that experience may be due to bile, phlegm or wind, to an imbalance of these humours or to their union, to a change in season, to some acute cause, or it may be the result of karma.[12]

The Buddha's teaching on karma is not, therefore, supposed to explain every ache and pain or moment of joy in our lives. However, despite these teachings being preserved in the Pali discourses, some contemporary Buddhists insist that everything that happens to anyone is because of their karma.[13] To hold this view is to suppose that karma and conditionality are the same thing, so that the whole universe is the working-out of past action. This interpretation puts too much emphasis on karma. It is more appropriate to understand the principle of karma as just *one* of the ways in which dependent arising works. We can describe these ways in terms of 'orders of conditionality':[14]

1. the *physical order of conditionality:* the regular workings of the physical world, with atoms, molecules and planets all arising on conditions, as described by physics, chemistry, etc.;
2. the *organic order of conditionality:* those patterns and laws by which living beings, from microbes to men, evolve and prosper, as described by biology, ecology, etc.;
3. the *subjective order of conditionality:* the workings of the mind, such as the subconscious processes of perception, memory and imagination, all arising on certain conditions, as described by psychology (which is not yet a very perfect science);
4. the *karmic order of conditionality:* the operation of karma, whereby skilful deeds lead to happiness, and unskilful deeds to pain; and
5. the transcendental order of conditionality: by which the spiritual path leads from *dukkha* to awakening, each step

arising in a progressive sequence and leading to human fulfilment.

Karma is therefore just one of the ways in which our experience arises dependent on conditions. If we are feeling depressed, for instance, it might have arisen through vitamin D deficiency (organic), or be related to childhood trauma (subjective), or be the result of past unwholesome actions now catching up with us (karma).

A second possible misunderstanding is that we can work out from our present experience what past action might now be coming to fruition. Karma does not work in this linear way. Any particular present experience is a composite consequence of many prior conditions, belonging to different orders of conditionality, and giving rise to effects through processes far too complex for any of us to perceive. It was in this sense that the fifth-century commentator Buddhaghosa described *paṭicca-samuppāda* as implying 'multiple fruits from multiple causes'.[15] Feeling depressed, for instance, might be the result of all sorts of conditions, among which are some past actions wholly or partially ripening; but some of these same conditions in combination with yet others might later create other experienced effects. Our actions flow into the stream of life-experience, like ripples radiating out and disappearing into the busy current. Sometimes past actions rebound upon us in recognizable ways, but generally speaking the situation is too infinite a tangle of influence for us to discern past karma at work. We might as well say that karma works in mysterious ways.

Karma as intention

While the brahmans understood karma as ritual action, and did not think about ethics, the Buddha's teachings on karma and rebirth appear superficially similar to Jain ideas about how karma keeps the soul trapped in samsara. However, the Buddha criticized the Jains for taking karma too literally. According to Jain tradition, for instance, even the accidental harming of living beings is bad karma, and eating a carrot is bad karma because vegetables are living beings. Pious Jains therefore sweep the path ahead of them to avoid stepping on ants, and filter their drinking water so as not to harm the microbes in it. Taken to its logical extreme, the Jain practice of *ahiṃsā* or harmlessness means to stop eating, for even vegetables are alive. Jain ascetics would starve themselves to death to free themselves from karma.[16] In contrast, the Buddha pointed out that it is the intention behind the action that makes it ethical or not. If, despite your mindfulness, you *accidentally* step on an ant, this is not an ethical matter – although, of course, you still might regret your carelessness in depriving an ant of its life. In short, the Buddha taught that what is important in our actions is the intention behind them:

> Monks, I say that karma is intention (*cetanā*); having intended, one does an action with the body, through speech, or with the mind.[17]

To talk of karma as intention marks a radical shift of emphasis. Now, what makes an action unskilful and leads to unpleasant results is the mental and emotional state of which it is the expression. Sangharakshita puts it like this:

> Deeds condense out of thought just as water condenses out of air. They are thought made manifest, and proclaim from the housetops of action only what has already been committed in the silent and secret chambers of the heart. One who commits an act of immorality thereby declares that he is not free from unwholesome states of mind.[18]

The experienced result of stealing, for instance, will be related to the state of selfish greed on which the act is based. If you give money to charity, your generous intention might have a very positive consequence on your own sense of self; but if the act was calculated to make you look ethically impressive then the result would be correspondingly hollow, though your generosity might in fact do some objective good.

The Buddha's teaching on karma therefore begins with the inner states, moods and feelings with which our actions start, and dependent on these states arise the consequences of our intentions within our own experience. More than anything else, the Buddha's teaching on karma is an encouragement to act ethically. If we make the appropriate effort to cultivate wholesome inner states, these not only lead to more ethical acts, words, and thoughts but also create the conditions for happier experiences. The Buddha spelled out this connection in the famous opening verses from the *Dhammapada*:

> Mind comes before experiences; mind is at their head;
> they arise from mind.
> If one speaks or acts with a degenerate mind,
> Then suffering follows, like a cartwheel behind the ox's
> tread.
>
> Mind comes before experiences; mind is at their head;
> they arise from mind.
> If one speaks or acts with a clear, radiant mind,
> Then happiness follows, like a shadow that never
> leaves.[19]

These verses are sometimes taken to suggest that the very existence of the world follows from the mind; but such an interpretation would be at odds with the practical and anti-metaphysical tenor of the Buddha's teaching. What is meant is that one's experience is profoundly coloured by the mind with which one sees it. To change this mind is to change one's experience of the world.

The Buddha's teaching that karma is intention has a profound implication. The Jains had a literal understanding of karma as a sort of stuff that keeps us in samsara. But if karma is really the intention behind an action, then karma is not literally something that clings to the soul. It is just a metaphor, a way of talking about how one's mental states are the condition for one's experience. The Buddha's teaching is that, while we are bound to experience, one way or another, the results of what we do, this does not mean that our lives are inescapably fixed by past actions. We can always choose to act in new and creative ways. By bringing awareness to experience, at the moment of contact and feeling, we can make space for creative, skilful decisions and actions, even in the midst of our own emotions. The Buddha's teaching on karma is therefore not a form of determinism, saying that everything in our lives is due to karma, but nor is it nihilism, according to which actions have no consequences.[20] It is a kind of middle way, acknowledging that we are always experiencing the results of past actions, but affirming that we can always choose what we do.

Whatever unskilful things we might have done, we can change our minds in the present moment, act in new ways, and in this way free ourselves from the results of past actions. This teaching is dramatically illustrated in the story of Aṅgulimāla, a serial killer whom the Buddha converted to his Dharma. Aṅgulimāla – or 'Finger Necklace' – terrorized an area in the kingdom of Kosala, killing his victims and threading their fingers into a grisly necklace. Through the charismatic power of the Buddha, however, Aṅgulimāla became a monk, and completely reformed his life. In so doing he overcame the past karma of his terrible evils, having only to endure stones thrown at him while on his almsround. His conversion is recorded in some verses:

> I used to be known as "Finger Necklace" and I have blood on my hands;
> But now look at my going for refuge! Uprooted is the course of my fate.
> Though due many bad rebirths for what I have done, my debt is paid;
> I enjoy my food, merely pelted as a result of past karma.[21]

In the realm of karma, the principle of conditionality therefore operates as a complex open system of conditions bringing various effects into being. Even the worst karma can be outweighed, for instance, by a sufficiently strong Dharma practice.[22]

Karma, defilements, and character

Since human beings are what they are largely through karma, changing the quality of our intentions changes the unfolding of our lives. There are intentions, characterized by greed, hate, and delusion, which give rise to unskilful actions, and those characterized by the opposites of greed, hate, and delusion, which give rise to skilful actions:

> Monks, there are these three sources (*nidānas*) for the arising of action. What are the three? Greed (*lobha*), hate (*dosa*), and delusion (*moha*) are sources for the arising of action. Monks, whatever action is done because of greed, born of greed, with greed as its source, and arising from greed, or done because of hate, born of hate, with hate as its source, and arising from hate, or done because of delusion, born of delusion, with delusion as its source, and arising from delusion – that action is unskilful (*akusala*), that action is blameworthy, that action results in pain, that action conduces to the arising of action, and that action does not conduce to the cessation of action. These, monks, are three sources for the arising of karma.
>
> But monks, there are also these three sources for the arising of action. What are the three? Non-greed (*alobho*), non-hate (*adosa*), and non-delusion (*amoha*) are sources for the arising of action. Monks, whatever action is done because of non-greed, born of non-greed, with non-greed as its source, and arising from non-greed, or done because of non-hate, born of non-hate, with non-hate as its source, and arising from non-hate, or done because of non-delusion, born of non-delusion, with non-delusion as its source, and arising from non-delusion – that action is skilful (*kusala*), that action is blameless, that action results in pleasure, that action conduces to the ceasing of action, and that action does not conduce to the arising of action. These, monks, are three more sources for the arising of action.[23]

Greed, hate, and delusion are known as 'defilements' (*kilesas*), because they spoil the purity of the mind, and 'afflictions' because they lead to suffering.[24] Greed signifies all our urges to grab, grasp, and get; hatred includes aversion, anger, and ill will; and delusion signifies the mental muddle and confusion by which we do not notice the state we are in. These are basic ways in which our emotional and mental experience is stirred up, heated, and muddied. When we act on such a basis, the outcome is unlikely to be good. Greed, hate, and delusion are likened to three fires with which human beings burn.[25] And they are called the three 'unskilful roots' (*akusala-mūlas*), because they are intentions that lack any proficiency in ethical understanding, and because from them grow and develop further unwholesome states and painful consequences.

Greed, hate, and delusion are three basic tendencies of the reactive mind. They lead to actions that will have painful consequences, and they lead to more entanglement in samsara – they 'conduce to the arising of action'. But there are three more basic tendencies: non-greed, non-hate, and non-delusion. These terms signify not only the absence of their opposites, but also positive qualities: generosity, love (*mettā*), and wisdom. From these 'skilful roots' (*kusala-mūlas*) – that is, roots of action informed by an understanding of ethics – grow all wholesome states leading to pleasant consequences. These qualities are the basic tendencies of the creative mind, and when our actions are infused with these qualities, we take energy out of the samsaric process, and make progress on the spiral path. Hence generosity, love, and wisdom 'conduce to the ceasing of action'.

Our reactive tendencies become established as habits when we keep enacting them out of basic ignorance. With ignorance as condition arise the formations (*saṅkhāras*) of body, speech, and mind – these are the first two of the twelve links of *paṭicca-samuppāda*. Not aware of how *dukkha* arises, we act from greed, hate, and delusion, and these actions become formations in both a passive and an active sense. Passively our actions are informed by previous actions, and actively they themselves form the patterns of our lives. Actions formed into a pattern of habits create character. However, when we act from generosity, love, and wisdom – tendencies of the creative mind – we not only develop positive character habits but also undo our more fixed and reactive tendencies.

Karma and ethics

It is sometimes said that karma is the basis of Buddhist ethics, but this is not quite true. The Buddhist approach to ethics follows from the perception that all living beings, just like ourselves, want to be happy and wish to avoid pain. This is another version of the 'golden rule' found in most world religions – do to others as you would have them do to you. The Buddhist version emphasizes empathy:

> All living beings are terrified of violence; all of them fear death.
> Comparing oneself with others, one should not do harm nor incite it.[26]

The basic Buddhist ethical precept is not to harm other beings, and the other precepts follow from non-harming.[27] The practice of Buddhist ethics involves cultivating this capacity for empathy until it becomes a vital sensitivity to others – until one 'lives trembling for (*anukampā*) the welfare of all living beings'.[28]

The connection between karma and ethics is that those actions with pleasant consequences are those that are in keeping with the precepts, and those actions with unpleasant consequences are those that take no notice of the well-being of others. Karma is the psychological background to Buddhist ethics:

> Monks, I say that there are three kinds of harming of living beings: conditioned by greed, conditioned by hate, and conditioned by delusion. I say that there are three kinds of taking the not-given ... three kinds of sexual misbehaviour ... three kinds of false speech ... three kinds of slanderous speech ... three kinds of harsh speech ... three kinds of meaningless chatter ... three

kinds of covetousness ... three kinds of ill will ... three kinds of wrong views .... Thus, monks, greed, hate, and delusion produce action and are origins (*nidānas*) of action. From the waning of greed, hate, and delusion is the waning of the origins of action.[29]

When we are under the influence of greed, hate, and delusion we are wrapped up in our own concerns, our own lives, our own selves. Actions originating in these states are not likely to take others into much account, and thus they are ethically unskilful. The skilful states of generosity, love, and wisdom, however, already imply awareness of our fellow beings, and the actions that originate in them will be characterized by a degree of empathy.

Actions are not skilful because they have pleasant consequences, but they have those consequences because they are skilful. The principle of karma therefore depends on Buddhist ethics, and it describes our psychology in such a way as to embody ethical values. If we do what is good for others, then there will also be a positive result for ourselves. Ultimately, the Buddha's teaching on karma is a means to persuade us to be ethical, as it encourages us to act skilfully. This comes across clearly in the Buddha's conversation with the Kālāmas, a people who were confused by the variety of religious views they had heard from different teachers. The Buddha's advice to them was to learn to trust their own judgement based on an appreciation of ethics:

> 'What do you think, Kālāmas, when greed, hate, or delusion arise in someone, do they bring well-being or harm?'
>
> 'Harm, lord.'
>
> 'And a greedy person, Kālāmas, overpowered by greed, or a hateful person, overpowered by hate, or a deluded person, overpowered by delusion, their mind overcome, harms living beings and takes the not-given, has love affairs, speaks falsely, and encourages others to do the same. Isn't all this for their long-term harm and pain?'

'Yes, lord.'

'What do you think, Kālāmas: are these things skilful (*kusala*) or unskilful (*akusala*)?'

'Unskilful, lord.'

'Culpable or blameless?'

'Culpable, lord.'

'Criticized by the wise or praised?'

'Criticized, lord.'

'When taken up and carried through, do they lead to harm and pain, or not? How does it seem to you?'[30]

The Buddha also asks the same questions regarding generosity, love, and wisdom: these qualities do not lead to unethical actions, they are skilful, blameless, praised by the wise, and they lead to well-being and happiness. We could think of these qualities as ethical virtues. The Buddha goes on to recommend that the Kālāmas develop loving-kindness (*mettā*) for all beings, as well as the other three *brahmavihāras* – compassion (*karuṇā*), gladness (*muditā*), and equanimity (*upekkhā*) – and these qualities are four distinctly Buddhist virtues, that is, four practical ways of making skilful intentions habitual in our lives.[31]

Ultimately, the Buddha's teachings on karma bring an ethical dimension into the patterns of conditionality we have already explored. Unskilful actions are based on ignorance, and contribute to the formations. Habitual formations of body, speech, and mind, characterized by greed, hate, and delusion, inevitably support the arising of craving at the moment of contact and feeling, and from craving arises the rest of the links belonging to samsara. Skilful actions, however, are ethical; they arise from wise attention to our experience as well as from faith in the Dharma, and hence from them arise further factors of the path. In short, the reactive mind is unskilful, while the creative mind acts skilfully, and enjoys the results.

Questions for Chapter Five

1. Why do you think that skilful actions give rise to pleasant experiences and unskilful actions to unpleasant experiences? Have you ever seen this process happening in your own experience?
2. The word 'karma' is used with different meanings in Buddhism and in popular culture. What are the different ways it is used and how are they related?
3. We can explore further the extent to which our lives are determined by what we do. Think of something in your life over which you feel that you have control, for example where you go on holiday, how you do your job, or how you spend your free time. Now draw a diagram (as in Chapter One) to show all the factors that influence your decisions and what happens. Do you have complete control?

   Now choose something over which you feel you have no control, for example climate change or some aspect of your job. Again, draw a diagram to show all the factors that contribute. Do you have influence over any of them?

   Is there anything in your life over which you have complete control? Is there anything over which you have no influence?
4. The fourth-century-BCE Greek philosopher Aristotle also recommended the cultivation of virtues as habits, as part of cultivating the best and happiest kind of life. In a work on ethics he writes:

   > Moral goodness is the result of habit... The moral virtues are engendered in us neither by nor contrary to nature; we are constituted by nature to receive them, but their full development in us is due to habit... we acquire the virtues by first exercising them, just as happens in the arts. Anything we have to learn to do we learn by the actual doing of it: people become builders by building and instrumentalists by playing instruments. Similarly we become just by performing just acts; self-controlled by performing self-controlled acts; brave by performing brave ones.[32]

   According to Aristotle, justice, self-control, wisdom, and courage are the four 'cardinal virtues'. What do you think might be Buddhist 'cardinal virtues'? Reflect on one virtue that you would like to develop. What small acts could you do to make this virtue a habit, and thus a part of you?

Chapter Six

Conditionality as Middle Way

Conditionality is not just a set of teachings or doctrines but also a way of thinking. In the light of the last chapter we could say that the Buddha's teaching on karma is a middle way between determinism, the idea that everything is due to past karma, and nihilism, the idea that nothing we do matters. We can always become aware and make creative, ethical choices, and hence change the course of our lives. In this chapter we will further explore the Buddha's middle way. Firstly, the Buddha described his lifestyle in a very practical sense as a middle way between the extremes of hedonistic indulgence and self-mortification. Secondly, the Buddha outlined how conditionality is a philosophical middle way between ideas of permanent existence and complete non-existence.

The middle way as a lifestyle

We saw in Chapter Two that once the Buddha had attained awakening on the bank of the Nerañjarā river, and had decided to teach the Dharma, he made his way to the Deer Park near Benares in order to share his discovery of awakening with five friends with whom he had once sought the truth. These were five ascetics with whom the Buddha had previously practised austerities. At first his erstwhile companions in the holy life chose not to welcome Gotama, regarding him as a backslider from their rigorous self-mortification. But seeing the glow of his skin and the serenity of his deportment, they spontaneously served him water and prepared him a seat, eager to hear what he had discovered.[1]

The Buddha then taught the five ascetics the First Sermon, culminating in the teaching of the four noble truths.[2] The sermon starts, however, with a presentation of the Buddhist path as a 'middle way' between two extremes:

> Thus have I heard. Once the Blessed One was living in Benares, at the Deer Park at Isipatana. Then the Blessed One addressed the group of five monks thus: 'There are these two extremes, monks, not to be followed by one who has gone forth. What two? That which is devotion to happiness and pleasure in sense-desires, which is common, vulgar, ordinary, ignoble, and not connected with the goal; and that which is devotion to self-mortification, which is painful, ignoble, and not connected with the goal. Avoiding both of these extremes, monks, is the middle way which the *tathāgata* has fully understood, which makes for knowledge and vision, for peace, realization, awakening, and nirvana. And what, monks, is the middle way? Just this noble eightfold path – right view, right intention, right speech, right action, right livelihood, right effort, right mindfulness, and right concentration. This, monks, is the middle way which the *tathāgata* has fully understood, which makes for knowledge and vision, for peace, realization, awakening, and nirvana.'[3]

The Buddha was letting his former companions know that, from his point of view, their attempts at self-mortification were painful and useless. However, the Buddha had already made it clear that a hedonistic lifestyle was equally to be avoided. The Buddha's middle way, we might say, is a creative solution to the problem of how to live a meaningful life; the problem being symbolized here in terms of unthinking hedonistic existence on the one hand, and a polarized rejection of it on the other.

These two extremes of lifestyle that need to be avoided by someone seeking awakening can be described as *hedonistic indulgence* and *self-mortification*. The middle way between these is the noble eightfold path, which is a summary of the Buddhist training in ethics, meditation, and wisdom. The middle way in this sense is not explicitly an application of dependent arising, but by exploring the issues raised by the two extremes of indulgence and self-mortification as strategies for human happiness, we will learn more about how the teaching of conditionality lies behind Buddhist practices. In short, the Buddhist path relies on giving rise to conditions that support growth and development according to the 'spiral path'. But to either side of this middle way lie lifestyle choices that do not create the conditions for the ending of *dukkha*.

The extremes of indulgence and self-mortification

Much of the traditional life story of the Buddha is an exemplification of the Dharma rather than a historical account of Gotama's life. With regard to the extreme of hedonistic indulgence, for instance, the Buddha told the following story about the refinement of his early life:

> My life was refined, monks, utterly refined, extremely delicate. My father even had lotus ponds made in our house – one in which blue lotuses bloomed, another in which red lotuses bloomed, another in which white lotuses bloomed, just for my sake. I used no sandalwood that was not from Benares; my turban was from Benares, and so were my tunic, my clothing, and my cloak. A white parasol was held over me day and night to prevent the touch of cold, heat, dust, dirt, and dew. I had three palaces: one for winter, one for summer, and one for the rainy season. In my rainy season palace, for the four months of the rainy season, entertained by all-women musicians, I did not come down from the palace.[4]

We can translate these images of exquisite refinement into contemporary terms. If you had a spacious detached house, designer clothes, a top-quality digital entertainment system, and a second home abroad for your holidays, would you want to venture out of your luxurious world?

The Buddha went on to observe, however, that such a pampered person, intoxicated with their health, youth and life, might well react to the sight of old age, illness and death with horror and disgust – an unfitting response to such inescapable aspects of the human condition. Hedonistic indulgence is 'common, vulgar, ordinary, and ignoble' for just this reason: it is a strategy for avoiding *dukkha* that does not help us come to any real understanding. The middle way involves recognizing and acknowledging *dukkha*, leaning into it with as much awareness as possible, in order to find the path that leads beyond *dukkha*. From the Buddhist point of view, hedonism is a poor strategy for finding true meaning in life. We can consider this in our own experience: when, in our moments of difficulty or weakness, we resort to sensual indulgence, does it help? What states or actions arise with indulgence as condition?

This does not mean, however, that the Buddhist path is without pleasure, and nor does it mean that Buddhists should not look for pleasure in their lives. There is rapture and bliss to be found in meditation, and also joy in the practice of ethics and generosity, a joy that comes from knowing that we are living well. Sangharakshita has even spoken of Buddhism as a 'higher hedonism'. He means that the rapture and bliss found in concentrated meditative states should be sought out and cultivated, for the *jhānas* (in Sanskrit, *dhyānas*), or states of meditative absorption, are purely wholesome, skilful states, with pleasant future consequences. The difference between hedonistic indulgence and this higher hedonism is that in the former one seeks pleasure through gratifying sense-desires, while in the latter the enjoyment is a welling up and overflowing of inner contentment.

If indulgence is the common and ordinary way in which human beings try to avoid *dukkha*, then self-mortification is a way in which spiritual seekers throughout history have attempted to conquer their passionate natures in search of freedom. Self-denial and willpower are the keynotes of this contrasting extreme, and once again the Buddha's life story furnishes us with illustrations of such trials. Prior to his awakening, the Buddha tried forcing his mind into submission, and then he tried stopping his breath. Then he tried fasting, and the graphic descriptions he gave of his asceticism have fascinated Buddhist sculptors since early times:

> My body became extraordinarily emaciated. Like knotted joints of grass or bamboo stems, so likewise were my limbs, just from eating so little. My backside was like a camel's hoof, just from eating so little. My ridged and furrowed backbone was like strung balls . . . My gaunt, wasted ribs were like the gaunt, wasted beams of an old barn . . . My eyes shone from deep in their sockets like the sparkle of water, way down deep in a well . . . Like the skin of an uncooked bitter gourd, shrivelled and withered in heat and wind, my scalp was shrivelled and withered . . . Thinking to rub my belly, I reached my backbone too; thinking to rub my backbone, I reached my belly too; in fact, my belly was stuck to my backbone, just from eating so little. Thinking to urinate or defecate I fell headlong in it, just from eating so little. To soothe my body, I stroked my limbs with my hands, but in stroking my limbs with my hands my body hair fell out, its roots rotted, because of eating so little.[5]

But Gotama concluded that for all this painful austerity he was no nearer putting an end to *dukkha*.

This is just one of the lurid stories the Buddha told about his former asceticism.[6] Perhaps a devotion to self-mortification of some sort is not so unusual a strategy by which people attempt to overcome what they perceive to be causes of *dukkha*. How often do we suppose that by devoting ourselves to a diet or an exercise regime we will make ourselves happier, overcome our weaknesses and push ourselves beyond what limits us? (This is not to deny that healthy eating and regular exercise are good for us.) How often do we seek in meditation practice to overcome what appears to imprison us with an attitude of wilful effort? The attitude of self-mortification involves siding with one part of ourselves against another part of ourselves that we perceive to be bad. Perhaps our capacity for such wilfulness has its occasional

Figure 4: *Fasting Buddha, Gandhāra period, 2nd–3rd c.* CE.

uses, but it also produces pain, internal conflict and unhappiness.

Self-mortification, then, is a 'painful and ignoble' way of life for the spiritual practitioner. The middle way, by contrast, involves setting up inner conditions, such as awareness and kindness, which naturally result in continuing integration and positivity. This does not exclude discipline and effort; in fact, these qualities are indispensable for progress. But the Buddha's middle way is not a harsh asceticism but a flexible responsiveness to what we need to work on. If we notice ourselves indulging in hedonism we might need to ask if this is really going to help; if we find a wilful forcefulness in our attitude we need to ease up. This middle way cannot be prescribed but consists in a balanced effort based on an intelligent application of conditionality.

The middle way between existence and non-existence

From lifestyle we leap to philosophy. We saw in Chapter One that, in conversation with Māluṅkyaputta, the Buddha refused to answer questions concerned with speculative metaphysics because they were irrelevant to the point of the Buddha's teaching – which is about *dukkha* and the end of *dukkha*. This does not mean, however, that it is pointless thinking about the nature of reality; it only means that the ultimate truth is not to be found through speculation. 'Right view' is in fact the first component of the eightfold path, meaning a set of ideas about the nature of reality that supports our ethics and meditation practice. One of the ways in which the Buddha defined right view was as a middle way. It consists in seeing that things, whether in the world or in our own experience, neither really exist nor are completely non-existent; things are dependently arisen, and this means that the way they exist transcends our preconceptions about them. In an important conversation with his disciple Kaccāyana, he explained it in this way:

> Venerable Kaccāyana approached the Blessed One, and, having exchanged greetings, sat to one side. Then, sitting to one side, the Venerable Kaccāyana said to the Blessed One:

'People say, "right view, right view", lord. But how should right view be defined?'

'Kaccāyana, this world mostly relies on the dichotomy of real existence and complete non-existence. But when one sees the origin of the world as it really is through right understanding, one does not have the idea of complete non-existence in relation to the world. Seeing the cessation of the world as it really is through right understanding, one does not have the idea of real existence in relation to the world. Kaccāyana, while this world is mostly bound up with attachment, clinging, and inclination, if one does not embrace or cling to attachments, mental fixations, inclinations, and tendencies, and one is not fixated on thinking about "my self", then one will not doubt that it is just *dukkha* arising and just *dukkha* ceasing. In this one's knowledge is not dependent on others. To this extent, Kaccāyana, is there right view.

'"Everything exists" is one extreme; "everything does not exist" is a second extreme. Avoiding both of these extremes, Kaccāyana, the *tathāgata* teaches Dharma by the middle (*majjhena dhammaṃ*): dependent on ignorance are the formations [and the rest of the *nidānas*].'[7]

It is important to bear in mind that the Buddha was not explaining philosophical theory to Kaccāyana. His middle way was a way of thinking about reality that helps bring an end to suffering.[8] The ideas of 'permanent existence' and 'complete non-existence' that most people are said to rely on are ways of thinking that we bring subconsciously to the world of ordinary experience. Thinking that things have definite, lasting existence or complete non-existence is a way in which we attempt to simplify the complexity of our experience and make it manageable. This might seem harmless enough, or even necessary to our lives. The problem, however, is that we are not usually aware of the emotional fixations and prejudices which are behind how we think. With our assumptions about 'existence' and 'non-existence' we seek to label and pin down things in our experience in accordance with our own interests, which the Buddha described as 'attachments, mental fixations, inclinations, and tendencies'.

Let us return to our example of stress to explore what this means. For someone who is experiencing stress, it is not just a philosophical matter to say that this stress is something that 'exists'. But let us just notice that 'stress' is a *word* as well as a thing, and it is only as a word that it exists independently, separated from other words, like 'tiredness' and 'overwork'. In reality, these things are closely interconnected. To the extent that we think in words, our ideas can suggest that the things we think about are more independent and self-existent than they actually are. Our desire to make our stress go away so that we are relieved of this source of pain can lead us to think of our stress as a kind of *thing* that now exists in a definite, solid way. Emotionally, we just want our stress to not exist, to disappear. And so we have existence and non-existence – we have the thought of this hateful stress reified into something fixed and solid in our experience, and we have the thought of no-stress, the removal of this stress, reified into an absence which we very much want.

At this point let us relax a little and remember how stress arises on conditions, and ceases when those conditions cease. Is it a thing, existing in its own right? No, because it depends upon other things. But even this talk of 'things' is misleading. Just because we have a word, *stress*, is there anything in our experience we can really label in this way? We experience stress not as one thing but as various symptoms such as insomnia, anxiety and a quickened heartbeat. Seeing 'stress' as these co-arising symptoms allows us to address each symptom appropriately. As we change the conditions, so the stress changes, until it becomes something else, something less of a problem. Wishing for *complete absence of stress* would not have been a productive strategy for achieving this change.

The right view that the Buddha describes as a middle way between the ideas of real existence and complete non-existence can be expressed by saying that our conditioned experience is best understood as a *process* without fixed existence in it, a matter of *becoming* rather than being. Normally, however, we take sides in the way that we think about 'things'. With our thoughts and words we superimpose ideas of real existence and complete non-existence on 'things' in our experience, and this leads to wrong views and bad decisions. The work situation that we are stressed about seems terrifying when it looms over us in all its real existence; but it looks much more manageable when we see it as a process consisting of component parts. The new gadget we have set our hearts upon glows in all its real desirability, though when we have it in our homes it takes its place as an imperfect machine in our complicated lives. Bearing the principle of conditionality in mind we can attend to our experience with an attitude of not siding with either extreme. We notice how things we are obsessed with are in fact dependent for their existence on other things, and that nothing goes away just by our wanting it to. Right view as a middle way transcends our usual tendency to want to pin things down in fixed ways.

Eternalism and annihilationism

To realize this middle way – to see that all our experience is a dependently arising process of becoming – is a hard-won spiritual achievement, equivalent to the stage of 'knowledge and vision of reality' on the spiral path. While we work towards it through our ethics and meditation practice, we can also begin to notice and work on some of our deeply held views about the nature of reality. 'Eternalism' and 'annihilationism' are two such views, corresponding to the extremes of 'real existence' and 'complete non-existence'. Is there an unchanging, eternal reality behind or beyond the changing world of appearances? Or is this fleeting world of transitory things all there is, such that death means complete annihilation? The Buddha's response to these great metaphysical questions illustrates how the middle way works as a subtle philosophical principle.

In the India of the Buddha's day a lively debate about what happens at death was carried on in terms of the *ātman* or 'Self', defined as the supposedly imperishable essence of who we are. The speculative thinkers of the Upaniṣads argued that the *ātman* was the core of subjective self-awareness – the sense that we have of an unchanging subjectivity as we experience all the various circumstances of our lives. They took it that this *ātman* survived the death of the physical body and was reborn; or if one had realized the true nature of the *ātman*, one merged with the *Brahman*, the true nature of things.[9] The Buddha called such a belief 'eternalism' (*sassatavāda*) – the view that who we really are, being imperishable, continues after death. Other materialist thinkers believed that since we are essentially physical beings, we cannot survive death, and there is no *ātman* that continues. The Buddha called this belief 'annihilationism' (*ucchedavāda*) – the view that who we really are just ends at death.[10]

The Buddha's own position on this matter is an application of conditionality. This world is a process of becoming. Consciousness, like everything else, arises dependent on other things, like a fire that burns dependent on fuel.[11] Thus consciousness is not an *ātman* or imperishable Self that continues or transmigrates (eternalism). But this does not mean that our lives and actions have no lasting significance or consequence (annihilationism). While the conditions that support existence endure, there will be the ripening of actions and re-becoming in samsara. Hence the Buddha taught rebirth as a process governed by karma, in the sense of the ethical quality of intentional actions. Whether we understand this teaching literally or metaphorically, it is a vision of existence as both meaningful and purposive, though having no unchanging or divine essence. It is a vision that throws us back on our own responsibility for what we will become.

For westerners reflecting on life and death, our thinking will probably be influenced by our own cultural versions of eternalism and annihilationism, which are theism and scientific materialism respectively. In the Christian version of theism there is 'one God, Father Almighty, maker of heaven and earth'.[12] This God is the eternal, unchanging creator of all things. Many westerners think of spirituality as by definition having to do with such an eternal divine being. However, the existence of God is incompatible with a universe in which all things have arisen through conditions. In the Buddha's day some held that Brahmā was the creator god. The Buddha was aware of such theistic beliefs, but rather than trying to disprove them, he made fun of them. For instance, he tells a story in which Brahmā is a powerful but deluded creator, thinking he has created other beings even though really they just appeared near him through the ripening of their past karma.[13]

Eternalist belief in God, however, is less prevalent these days, at least in Europe, than its annihilationist counterpart, scientific materialism. Such a view, deriving from the scientific revolution beginning in the seventeenth century, excludes the idea of a creator god and envisions human beings as products of the machinery of material evolution, without any higher destiny. The late-nineteenth-century thinker Arthur Balfour gave vivid expression to this vision of existence:

> Man, so far as natural science by itself is able to teach us, is no longer the final cause of the universe, the heaven-descended heir of all the ages. His very existence is an accident, his story a brief and transitory episode in the life of one of the meanest of the planets. Of the combination of causes which first converted a dead organic compound into the first progenitors of humanity, science, indeed, as yet knows nothing. It is enough that from such beginnings famine, disease and mutual slaughter, fit nurses of the future lords of creation, have gradually evolved, after infinite travail, a race with conscience enough to feel that it is vile, and intelligence enough to know that it is insignificant. We survey the past, and see that its history is of blood and tears, of helpless blundering, of wild revolt, of stupid acquiescence, of empty aspirations. We sound the future, and learn that after a period, long compared with the individual life, but short indeed compared with the divisions of time open to our investigation, the energies of our system will decay, the glory of the sun will be dimmed, and the earth, tideless and inert, will no

> longer tolerate the race which has for a moment disturbed its solitude.[14]

This wonderful evocation of spiritual pessimism is not supposed to represent the whole effect of modern science on our outlook, only to give expression to the outlook to which the world view of science might give rise. Recent developments in evolutionary theory and neuroscience suggest that consciousness is by no means just a brief and pointless by-product of the accidental combination of atoms. Instead, consciousness appears to be an emergent quality of the neural complexity of the human brain – perhaps the most complex organism in the universe. And conscious self-awareness seems to have been enormously advantageous to evolving *Homo sapiens*. It is as if the universe had been waiting for consciousness to emerge. On the other hand, we might like to consider to what degree the world view of science predisposes us to live in a world stripped of myth and higher meaning, and hence ready to believe in consumerism, happy to take on *dukkha* with technology.

Applying conditionality as the middle way in our western context, we might say that we were not created by God nor are we just soulless conglomerates of complicated molecules. Both of these positions, from the Buddhist perspective, are extreme views. Arising on conditions, human beings, we might say, are the product of millions of years of evolution, and consciousness is life become aware of itself. There is no need to posit the existence of a creator god, as conditionality is a powerful enough principle to explain the evolution of the universe. The self-conscious humanity that has arisen through evolution is not, however, just a product of material complexity. Although scientists have discovered much about the processes by which the brain functions, this does not imply that consciousness can be reduced to brain activity. To be conscious is to be the knowing subject of experience, and subjectivity cannot be explained merely by identifying its objective conditions. To put it another way, *dukkha* is not a product of brain activity, and although the effects of meditation on the brain can be observed, the effort to cultivate mindfulness and loving-kindness is made by existing individuals, not by brains.

Questions for Chapter Six

1. How different do you think the ordinary household lifestyle of a contemporary westerner might be from the lifestyle of someone of the Buddha's time and place? Can you think of contemporary kinds of lifestyle that are polarized rejections of ordinary life? How do you envisage a contemporary Buddhist lifestyle that is a middle way between ordinary life and a rejection of it?
2. What do indulgent and self-mortifying attitudes towards food look like in our culture? Which one of them do you tend towards? What would be a middle way?
3. Do you tend towards eternalism or annihilationism? How do you think that someone's views on whether or not we exist after death affect how they will live their life?

Chapter Seven

The Nature of Existence

Now that we have explored how *paṭicca-samuppāda* is the fundamental formulation of the Dharma, and seen how conditionality underlies the Buddha's practical teaching concerning *dukkha*, as well as the path to awakening, ethics and the middle way, we will step back from the contents of experience to study its fundamental nature as dependently arisen. According to the Buddha, seeing dependent arising means seeing the Dharma, the truth of how things really are. This means that everything is dependently arisen; everything is conditioned (except nirvana). Everything in our experience – in the world or in our minds – arises on certain conditions, and will cease when those conditions cease. This is Buddhist metaphysics, that is, the Buddhist account of the nature of reality. I do not mean speculative metaphysics, the product of mere abstract thought, which the Buddha considered irrelevant. Rather, it is a metaphysical vision of the nature of things sprung from the Buddha's direct realization of the truth, which we might take on faith (*saddhā*) for the sake of ourselves coming to know the Dharma.

If everything is conditioned, three fundamental characteristics or 'marks' (*lakkhaṇas*) of existence follow. Firstly, all conditioned things are *anicca*, 'impermanent', since they completely depend on the conditions which produce them, all of which are also impermanent. Secondly, all conditioned things are *dukkha*, since no permanent satisfaction or fulfilment can be found in what is impermanent. And, thirdly, all things whatever, including nirvana, lack an enduring essence or selfhood; all things whatever are *anattā*, 'without self'. In this chapter we will meditate on these three characteristics of existence.

All conditioned things are impermanent and unsatisfactory

Everything around us is dependently arisen (*paṭicca-samuppanna*). The trees in the park have grown from seeds, and continue to depend on water and sunlight. The earth itself, we now believe, came into being around 4.5 billion years ago along with the rest of the solar system, and will continue in existence as long as its conditions persist. Even the atoms of which everything is made came into existence after the universe began, and may not last forever. In this conditioned existence, everything arising is conditioned, and at the same time is a condition upon which other things arise. The Buddha called such conditioned things, which are also conditions for other things, *saṅkhāras*, or 'formations'.[1] As the second *nidāna*, formations signify the tendencies and volitions in our experience that arise with ignorance, and which are the condition for consciousness and the rest of the links. Such formations include habits and volitions – tendencies of the reactive mind that are the result of past karma and which are themselves new karma. However, the Buddha also used the word *saṅkhāra* to refer more broadly to all conditions and conditioned things; hence *sabbe saṅkhārā aniccā* – 'all formations are impermanent'. In the words of the *Dhammapada*:

> 'All conditioned things are impermanent' – seeing this
> with wisdom
> one wearies of suffering. This is the path to purity.[2]

The impermanence of conditioned things means that everything is subject to change. In a sense, reality itself is change; reality is a process. Later Buddhists took this metaphysical perspective literally, and developed a doctrine of universal flux, saying that behind appearances was a continual succession of states, arising and passing with inconceivable rapidity. But the Buddha's teaching concerned what we can directly observe:

> Monks, there are these three conditioned-characteristics of what is conditioned (*saṅkhata*). What are the three? Arising is to be discerned; passing away is to be discerned; and change in what continues to exist is to be discerned. These three, monks, are the three conditioned-characteristics of what is conditioned.[3]

Intellectually, at least, impermanence is not hard to see. Emotionally, however, it can be more difficult. When we are in love we refuse to believe that it is a transient state, and when we feel depressed it is notoriously hard to remember that everything changes.

The experience of change is an age-old subject for poets, observing, bemoaning or resisting the relentless passing of time. Buddhist poets too have written of impermanence, but the mood of such poems is a brave, bold stare into the eyes of the demon. Here is a poem by the Chinese Buddhist poet Han-shan:

> You have seen the blossoms among the leaves;
> Tell me, how long will they stay?
> Today they tremble before the hand that picks them;
> Tomorrow they await someone's garden broom.
> Wonderful is the bright heart of youth,
> But with the years it grows old.
> Is the world not like these flowers?
> Ruddy faces, how can they last?[4]

For Buddhism, the impermanence of formations is more of a mood than a fact. Part of this mood is a clear-eyed appreciation of how things are in this moment, knowing that things will change, and that the complex conditions of this moment will last but a spell. Now Sangharakshita:

> Thrown on the white wall
> Shadows of flowers
> Have nothing to say.[5]

One might describe the poetry of impermanence in terms of the aesthetics of mindfulness. The practice of awareness and of meditation produces a certain way of looking at the world, which is highly sensitive while keeping a mindful distance.[6]

As we observe the changing world and our own lives passing, we realize that we have no time to lose if we are to make progress on the spiritual path. Buddhists have looked hard at their crumbling bodies, to shatter the illusion of endless life. The following verses describe the reflections of the old nun Ambapālī, once a beautiful courtesan and friend of the Buddha:

> Black as the black colour of bees were my curls; age
> makes them like hemp-bark fibres – *words of one who speaks only truth.*
>
> Scented like a basket full of flowers was my head; age
> makes it smell like dog's hair – *words of one who speaks only truth.*
>
> Like wonderful jewels my eyes were dark and large; age
> has long ruined their beauty – *words of one who speaks only truth.*
>
> My singing was as sweet as the wood-wandering nightingale; age
> finds me faltering at each note – *words of one who speaks only truth.*[7]

The realism of Ambapālī's clear-sighted meditation on her ageing body reminds us how growing old is unavoidable, and how death hangs over our dependently arisen existence. This aspect of impermanence leads to another mood: that of spiritual urgency (*saṃvega*).[8] The fleeting nature of all conditioned things prompts us to cease searching for satisfaction in ephemera, and to look for that which truly satisfies. We can use the moods of impermanence to develop wisdom or insight (*paññā*) into the nature of existence. Doing so, we might become aware of the *dukkha* inherent in our situation, and hence disenchanted with the ordinary round. So the path begins, and ends with liberation from reliance on all this inconstancy:

> Impermanent, alas, are formations, of a nature to arise
> and pass away;
> Having arisen, they cease again – the assuaging of all this
> is bliss.[9]

Impermanent things are by their nature unreliable, and it is only by knowing and seeing what does not change that this unreliability is assuaged. Nevertheless, impermanence is in a sense a blessing, since if things were not impermanent we could not change and make progress on the spiritual path. But while we continue to seek satisfaction in conditioned things, we will encounter frustration. It is in this sense that *sabbe saṅkhārā dukkhā*, 'all formations are unsatisfactory':

> 'All formations are unsatisfactory' – seeing this with
> wisdom
> one wearies of suffering. This is the path to purity.[10]

The suffering referred to here may not be what we think of as actual pain; we may go years without acute suffering. Again, we are talking more of a mood – of an existential discontent rooted in the nature of the conditioned world, in which our aspirations are infinite even while we live in these very finite bodies.[11] Hence the Buddha distinguished three kinds of *dukkha*:

(i) the painfulness of pain (*dukkha-dukkhatā*), of broken bones and broken hearts;
(ii) the unsatisfactoriness of formations (*saṅkhāra-dukkhatā*), the existential mood that comes from observing arising and passing away; and
(iii) the discontent born of change (*vipariṇāma-dukkhatā*), the disappointment that comes from the fact that precious things do not stay, not even love or happiness, but are lost and have to be sought over again.[12]

It may seem dispiriting to consider that *dukkha* is so intertwined in the nature of things. The truth is, however, that to open ourselves to the nature of conditioned things as being unsatisfactory brings us closer to reality. We will be less inclined to believe in our fantasies of perfection. Instead, our vivid awareness of unsatisfactoriness can become the condition for faith in the Buddhist path.

All things are without self

The impermanence of conditioned things is a teaching that we have to acknowledge, albeit grudgingly, as being in accordance with experience. But the Buddha's teaching on *anattā*, or 'not-self', is another matter. *Sabbe dhammā anattā*, 'all things are without self':

> 'All things are not-self' – seeing this with wisdom
> one wearies of suffering. This is the path to purity.[13]

To understand the teaching of 'not-self', we have to know about this 'self' that the Buddha contradicted. Many of the Buddha's religious contemporaries conceived of their spiritual quest in terms of a search for the *ātman* or 'self', the imperishable essence of who we are. In the Upaniṣads this *ātman* is said to be identical with *Brahman*, the one reality behind all the variety in the manifest world, and the Upaniṣads maintain that this *ātman* can be found through religious practices. The Buddha's teaching of *anattā* (in Sanskrit, *an-ātman* – that is, 'not-*ātman*') denies this conception of the spiritual life. According to the Buddha, no imperishable true essence of identity can be found anywhere. Instead, according to the teaching of *paṭicca-samuppāda*, existence is an ever-changing flow of states, physical and mental – a process of becoming. The self, like everything else, is a process.

Most of us ordinarily assume that we exist as a self, an ego, an 'I'. It seems obvious that the same self that existed yesterday will exist tomorrow, and that we exist more or less as the same person from our earliest experiences until we die. The ancient Indian conception of the *ātman* as a permanent self is a reification of such ordinary assumptions. The Buddha's denial of this belief was difficult to understand even in his own day, as shown by the following interchange between the Buddha and a wanderer named Vacchagotta, who is often represented in the suttas as rather perplexed about difficult teachings:

anattā

(in Pali; in Sanskrit *anātman*) means simply 'not-self'. As a characteristic of conditioned existence, *anattā* refers to the absence of a substantial and permanent centre to experience. To have insight into *anattā* means to realize through personal knowledge how all of our experience is made up of processes – physical, emotional and mental – and that the sense of 'I', 'me' and 'mine' is a deep-rooted habit which is ultimately a mistake. Nevertheless, although the Buddha and the arahants know the truth of 'not-self', they still use words like 'I', 'me' and 'mine', to refer to their actions, feelings and thoughts. They do this in accordance with conventional language, but they do not make the mistake of supposing that words like 'I' or 'mine' refer to anything that really exists

Vacchagotta the wanderer approached the Blessed One, and, having exchanged greetings, sat to one side. Then Vacchagotta the wanderer, sitting to one side, said this to the Blessed One:

'Now, master Gotama, is there a self (*attā*)?'

When this was said, the Blessed One remained silent.

'But, master Gotama, does the self not exist?'

A second time the Blessed One remained silent, and Vacchagotta the wanderer got up and left. Then, not long after Vacchagotta the wanderer had left, Venerable Ānanda said this to the Blessed One:

'Why, lord, did you not answer the wanderer Vacchagotta's questions?'

'Ānanda, had I, being asked by Vacchagotta the wanderer, "is there a self?", answered that the self exists, that would have been to agree with those ascetics and brahmans who are eternalists. Ānanda, had I, being

> asked by Vacchagotta the wanderer, "does the self not exist?", answered that the self does not exist, that would have been to agree with those ascetics and brahmans who are annihilationists.
>
> 'Ānanda, had I, being asked by Vacchagotta the wanderer, "is there a self?", answered that the self does exist, would that be consonant with the arising of the knowledge that "all things are not-self"?'
>
> 'Certainly not, lord.'
>
> 'Ānanda, had I, being asked by Vacchagotta the wanderer, "does the self not exist?", answered that the self does not exist, wouldn't the bewildered wanderer Vacchagotta be even more confused, thinking, "I used to have a self, but now it doesn't exist"?'[14]

What Vacchagotta wanted was a nice clear teaching about the *ātman*. But this discourse shows the Buddha not wanting to mislead him. The *anattā* teaching certainly means that the self is not a permanent and imperishable essence of the person. But it does not mean that the self is completely non-existent. The sense of self is based on the perception of various specific and unique physical and mental processes that constitute who we are as persons. The not-self teaching therefore implies a middle way between an eternalist view and the view that there is no self at all.

Our everyday assumption that 'I' exist is therefore not entirely wrong. There is a continuity of self in the sense of a process of dependently arisen states. In terms of the practicalities of the spiritual life there is no question of trying to 'get rid' of the ego, or anything like that, as if we would be enlightened if only we had no self. As Sangharakshita comments:

> The ego is no more than the tendency to absolutize one's present state of being. It is not a thing but a faulty interpretation. The individual is there in a process of continuous change and therefore of ever-present

> potential development; delusion may also be there, in the form of a belief in a fixed, unchanging self or essence or soul. But that fixed, unchanging self or essence or soul or ego is not there; it never was, and it never will be. And because it isn't there, one can't do anything with it – get rid of it, go beyond it, or whatever. The best thing to do as far as the ego is concerned is just to forget about it.[15]

In fact, for most of us, the early stages of the spiritual life consist in building up a healthier, more integrated sense of self. Through the practice of ethics and meditation we can develop sufficient emotional buoyancy and robustness to look deeper into the mystery of what a human being is.

Once we are ready to probe the mystery, the Buddha's recommendation to his followers was to analyse experience in terms of five constituents (*khandhas*):

(i) **form** (*rūpa*): our physical body and the external reality we encounter, whether seen, heard, smelled, tasted, or touched, such as the physical presence of a book seen with the eye, held in the hand, and read with the mind;
(ii) **feeling** (*vedanā*): the hedonic response to that encounter, experienced as pleasant, painful, or neutral, such as responses to words on a page;
(iii) **perception** (*saññā*): the recognizing and labelling of the various components of any experience, such as the word 'book', and ideas like 'Buddhism';
(iv) **formations** (*saṅkhāras*): everything that we bring to an experience, such as the ability to read, and our habitual ways of thinking about ideas;
(v) **consciousness** (*viññāṇa*): the conscious subject of experience, such as our awareness of reading a book, turning the page, and so on.[16]

These five constituents represent the Buddha's analysis of what is involved in being a person. The point of the analysis is to draw attention to how we are made up of constituents, none of which can be considered a 'self'. As the nun Vajirā declares:

technical terms in Buddhism

khandha

(in Pali; in Sanskrit *skandha*) means literally a 'mass' or 'bulk' – as in 'thus arises this whole mass (*khandha*) of *dukkha*' at the end of the formulation for the arising of the twelve *nidānas*. The body of an elephant is a *khandha*, as is the trunk of a tree. When the Buddha describes the human person as made of five *khandhas*, he means that we are just five masses of different things: body (*rūpa*), feeling (*vedanā*), perception (*saññā*), formations (*saṅkhārā*) and consciousness (*viññāṇa*). The five *khandhas* have been translated as 'heaps' and 'aggregates', but we have used 'constituent' as it gives the sense of a 'component part'. Human beings are not just random 'heaps' but organisms very precisely constructed by nature to think and feel – and yet we are without a permanent self.

> Just as we use the word 'chariot' to name a collection of parts,
> So by convention we say 'creature' when the *khandhas* are present.[17]

The Buddha presented this analysis not as an abstract doctrine but as a tool for us to investigate who or what we really are.

In a discourse traditionally regarded as the 'Second Sermon', the Buddha presents his teaching on *anattā* to his first five disciples in the form of two arguments. Firstly, he asks whether we have any control over the five constituents:

> At one time the Blessed One was living at Benares, at the Deer Park at Isipatana. Then the Blessed One addressed the group of five monks:
>
> 'Monks,' he said.
>
> 'Sir,' those monks replied to the Blessed One. And the Blessed One said:
>
> 'Form, monks, is without self. If form were self, then it would not be disposed to illness, and with regard to

> form it would be possible to say, "may my form be like this, may my form not be like that." But, monks, because form is without self, then form is disposed to illness, and it is not possible to say with regard to form, "may my form be like this, may my form not be like that." [And the same with feeling, perception, formations, and consciousness.]'

If the constituents are not in our control – if our bodies get ill, or we get miserable or stressed – does it make any sense to say that they are my 'self'? If 'I' am not able to dispose my body, feelings, perceptions, formations, or consciousness as I want, are they really what 'I' am? Secondly, the Buddha asks if the constituents are permanent or not:

> 'What do you think, monks – is form [feeling, perception, formations, or consciousness] permanent or impermanent?'
>
> 'Impermanent, lord.'
>
> 'And what is impermanent – is that unsatisfactory (*dukkha*) or pleasing (*sukha*)?'
>
> 'Unsatisfactory, lord.'
>
> 'And what is impermanent, unsatisfactory, and subject to change – is it appropriate to regard it thus: "this is mine, I am this, this is my self"?'
>
> 'Certainly not, lord.'
>
> 'Therefore, monks, whatever form [feeling, perception, formations, or consciousness] there is – past, future, or presently arisen, internal or external, coarse or subtle, inferior or excellent, far away or nearby – all that form [etc.] should be seen with right insight as it really is in this way: "this is not myself, I am not this, this is not my self".'

The five constituents are impermanent and dependently arisen – they are changing processes – and therefore they cannot be the unchanging *ātman*. But if the *ātman* cannot be found in the five constituents, where else can it be found? The discourse concludes with a description of how insight into the not-self characteristic leads to full liberation:

> 'Monks, a noble disciple, seeing like this, having studied it, becomes disenchanted with form [feeling, perception, formations, and consciousness]. Disenchanted, one becomes dispassionate, and through dispassion one is liberated. When one is liberated, there is knowledge that one is liberated. One understands that birth is destroyed, the holy life has been lived, what was to be done has been done, and that there is no further existence like this.'
>
> When the Blessed One had spoken, the group of five monks were delighted, and they rejoiced at the teaching of the Blessed One. Indeed, while this explanation was being made, the minds (*citta*) of the group of five monks were liberated from the pollutants through non-clinging.[18]

The Buddha's teaching of *anattā* is certainly designed to undercut any assumption that there is a permanent self in or behind the changing constituents of our experience. But it is also designed to undermine our ordinary habit of thinking of ourselves as a fixed identity, as an 'I' and 'me' who is quite separate from others. In the ordinary unawakened state, the familiar sense of 'I', 'me' and 'mine' amounts to an ignorant grasping (*upādāna*) onto the constituents.[19] Most of us identify, to some extent, with what we experience. For instance, the sound (*form*) of a certain person's voice (a *perception*) can trigger an unpleasant *feeling*, to which we respond, for instance by avoiding having to see or speak to that person (*formation*). And we are consciously aware (*consciousness*) all of the time of what we are doing, experiencing it something like this: 'God, I hate him – even the sound of his voice makes my skin crawl; I'm staying here until he's gone.' By ignorant identification with the constituents, the sense of self creates itself. We find ourselves hanging around somewhere, waiting for the person we dislike to move on. We might even notice how ridiculous the situation is. If we analyse the experience in terms of the five constituents (while we're waiting for him to go), we notice that they are impermanent and dependently arisen. It isn't really 'me' who doesn't want to meet him, it's just strong aversion happening. Do we want to live our lives like this – believing in our strong emotions, whatever the cost to our dignity? Why not start to let go, and face up to life, trusting in our values and our commitment to truth? Of course, the task of letting go of our deep-seated grasping to the constituents is difficult and takes a long time: to experience *anattā* is like trying to see through our own mind's magical illusion. Even if we have faith in the Buddha's teaching, we will still find ourselves caught up in the drama of the ego, with all the ups and downs of its never-ending story.

It is only when we reach the stage of knowing and seeing reality (the factor of the spiral path arising from concentration) that we see the self for what it is. With the arising of insight the fetter of 'personality view' (*sakkāya-diṭṭhi*) is abandoned.[20] However, even after the arising of insight, a sense of self remains in the form of the residual conceit 'I am'. The monk Khemaka, asked by his fellow monks about whether he still thought of any of the constituents as his self, told them that, although he knew and understood that there was no self, he still found a sense of 'I am' remaining, like the scent of a flower, or the fragrance of soap powder on clean clothes.[21] For those of us at the start of the Buddhist path, therefore, the teaching of not-self represents a direction or an implication of conditionality. Our task is to bring creative states of mind into being, and we will find that, as we make some progress, there is less a sense of an 'I' or a 'me' trying to get somewhere, though at the same time more of a sense of clarity and purpose.

Proliferation and conflict

It is relatively easy to admit that conditioned existence is impermanent and unsatisfactory, but the not-self teaching goes more against the grain of ordinary human experience. We might wonder how, if not-self-ness is a characteristic of existence, such a persistent illusion as the sense of 'I' and 'me' arose. And, moreover, what does it mean to do without it? These are difficult questions, but the Buddha went some way towards answering them with another nidāna chain that shows the arising of the sense of self as well as the conflict and strife that arises between people.

But first, to set the scene, another story: the Buddha was once approached by a brahman who was angry because a young man of that brahman's clan had converted to the Buddha's teaching. The angry brahman 'insulted and criticized the Blessed One with harsh and discourteous words.' But the Buddha questioned the man as follows:

> 'What do you think, brahman; do your friends and companions, family members and relatives come to visit you?'
>
> 'Yes, Mr Gotama, sometimes my friends and companions, family members and relatives come to visit me.'
>
> 'What do you think, brahman; do you serve them meals, snacks, or refreshments?'
>
> 'Yes, Mr Gotama, I serve them meals, snacks, and refreshments.'
>
> 'Now, brahman, if they did not accept them, to whom would they belong?'
>
> 'If they did not accept them, they would still belong to me.'
>
> 'Likewise, brahman, you insult someone who does not insult back, you taunt someone who does not get annoyed, you quarrel with someone who does not quarrel, and I do not accept any of it. Therefore, brahman, it belongs to you! Brahman, trading insults, paying back taunts and arguing back – all this would be

> like joining you to eat a meal. I will not join you to eat such a meal. Keep your insults, brahman; they belong only to you!'[22]

No doubt at some point we have all found ourselves the victim of verbal abuse. How did it feel to be insulted, taunted, and abused? Putting aside whether the insult was justified, most of us would admit that we took the insult personally; we felt stung and hurt, and reacted strongly in one way or another.

This is ego. This is what the Buddha did not have. His refusal of the angry brahman's insults was not just restraint but complete lack of reactivity. This is because an awakened person's experience is not subject to a certain kind of psychological process by which the reactive mind asserts and defends its sense of 'I' and 'me'. This process is called *papañca*, or 'proliferation'.[23] If someone is late for a meeting that you're attending, for instance, little thoughts might start spinning up out of your feelings of boredom or frustration. After fifteen minutes, the little thoughts have become self-justifying rage at your friend's discourtesy. When they turn up, and you barely restrain yourself from an outburst, you discover that they had been using their first aid skills after witnessing a bicycle accident, but still they express their sincere regret for being late; you suddenly see the delusional quality of your mental and emotional proliferation.

In the narrative opening of a discourse that discusses *papañca*, the Buddha is challenged by a slightly aggressive Sakyan called Daṇḍapāṇi to state his doctrine. The Buddha pointedly replies:

> Friend, the sort of teaching by which one does not contend with anyone in the world . . . and by which perceptions no longer persistently recur for that brahman living unattached to sense-pleasures, free from doubt, with remorse removed, having no craving for existence or non-existence – such is my teaching, friend, and such have I declared.[24]

Later, however, the Buddha's disciple Mahākaccāna gives a fuller explanation of the Buddha's cryptic utterance:

> Dependent on the eye and form [on the ear and sounds, on the nose and odours, on the tongue and tastes, on the body and touchables, on the mind and mental objects] arises eye-consciousness [and so on]. The conjunction of the three is contact. With contact as condition arises feeling. What one feels, that one perceives. What one perceives, that one thinks about. What one thinks about, that one proliferates about. With what one proliferates about as the source, conceptual and perceptual proliferation assail one in terms of forms cognizable with the eye [sounds cognizable with the ear, and so on], in relation to past, present, and future.[25]

Some of this series of conditions is familiar from the twelvefold *nidāna* chain. The links from consciousness to contact are here represented by a simpler psychological account of perception, in which the condition for contact is described simply as the conjunction between sense object, sense organ and consciousness. With contact as its condition arises feeling: these, of course, are the fifth and sixth links of the twelve *nidānas*.

After feeling, however, this teaching describes the development of a different series of experiences, now described not as impersonal events but as implying a participating subject. What one feels, one perceives, one thinks about and one proliferates about. The ego conjures itself out of a primary reality of felt experience by perceiving itself feeling ('I like' or 'I don't like'), and then thinking over that very experience. Proliferation now sets in, the mind developing its sense of self through a repertoire of reactions, and developing the story of itself as having connected experiences stretching from past through the present and into the future, in relation to the sensory world. Instead of me having thoughts, my thoughts are now having me. All this, however, is the manifestation of a secondary reality on or over a basic felt sense, which is present though obscured by what has been proliferated.[26] This does not mean that all thinking is proliferation. The point is that most of our thinking activity is just reactive proliferation. This account of proliferation is a parallel to the account in the twelve *nidānas* of the emergence of craving and clinging from feeling. While craving is primarily affective, proliferation is cognitive. The proliferation sequence of *nidānas* is a complementary perspective on how *dukkha* arises in experience.

We can go some way to understanding this teaching by considering the role of imagination in experience. The human power of imagination allows us to predict the future, recall the past, and fly ourselves around the world on the wings of thought. But when this vast power of imagination is employed by the reactive mind, it amplifies our greed, heightens our hatreds, and multiplies our delusion. Only human beings are capable of persecution and torture, and of plotting mass destruction. Proliferation is reactive imagination, and the proliferated world of the ego is the outward projection of our personalized reactivity.

By contrast, an awakened being is *nippapañca*, 'without proliferation'. With complete mindfulness, such a person is no longer prey to the proliferative tendency, but remains aware of primary reality as it is, without reacting to it. Living with awareness in the 'gap' between feeling and craving, the series of links leading from feeling to proliferation ceases. The Buddha describes such a person as a 'sage at peace' (*muni santa*). Of this sage, he says:

> the sage at peace is not born; not being born, such a one does not die, is not disturbed, and is without desire. For there is nothing by which he might be born; not being born, what will age? Not ageing, what will die? Not dying, what will be disturbed? Not being disturbed, for what would such a one long?[27]

The person without proliferation has clearly left ordinary human existence, with its birth, ageing, and death, far behind. And yet we know that the Buddha 'died' in a bodily sense. I suggest that these words are an attempt to describe the subjective experience of a liberated person. This means that there is an experience of the Deathless, even though everyone must 'die'. If this appears not to make sense, it may be a reminder that dependent arising is deep and profound.

The conditioned and the unconditioned

The nature of conditioned existence is impermanent, unsatisfactory, and without self; but it would be a sorry tale if this was the whole story. Whereas *sabbe saṅkhārā* – 'all formations' – are impermanent and unsatisfactory, *sabbe dhammā* – 'all things' – are not-self. The distinction is important. The term *dhammā* is wider than *saṅkhārā*, for as well as including all formations (*saṅkhārā*), which are conditioned states (*saṅkhata dhammā*), it also includes nirvana, which is the one unconditioned 'thing' or state (*asaṅkhata dhamma*). And while nirvana, like everything else in existence, is characterized as not-self, it is also permanent, unchanging, ultimate bliss.[28]

If nirvana is the unconditioned, this could be taken to mean that it is *outside* of conditionality; but this cannot be the case. We recall that the Buddha identified *paṭicca-samuppāda* both with himself and with the Dharma; he does not say that nirvana is something above or beyond them. Moreover, the Buddha made clear that he did not teach that anything arises without a condition.[29] So what did it mean for the Buddha to talk of the 'unconditioned'? The answer is that the Buddha presents the unconditioned as what is left when the conditions that lead to *dukkha* have ceased. It is a purely negative description of a state beyond words or concepts, something that is an experience but at the same time not an experience in any familiar sense of the term.[30]

If this sounds obscure and abstract, a bit of etymology might help. The word *asaṅkhata*, which I have translated 'unconditioned', might more literally be translated 'uncompounded'.[31] An 'uncompounded' experience would be one that is completely simple and pure, not defiled by any adventitious states or conditions. That this is what the Buddha meant by the term 'unconditioned' is shown by how he invited his followers to think about it in terms of what it does not contain:

> Monks, I will teach you the unconditioned and the path going to the unconditioned, so listen. What is the unconditioned? The destruction of greed, the destruction of hate, the destruction of delusion – this, monks, is what is called the unconditioned.[32]

The path going to the unconditioned is subsequently described in several ways: it is mindfulness of the body, insight meditation, the eightfold path, and so on. Moreover, in later discourses it becomes clear that *asaṅkhata* is a synonym for nirvana, other synonyms for which are *nippapañca*, 'the unproliferated', the Deathless, the unageing, and the refuge (*saraṇa*).[33]

The unconditioned, then, is the state that is uncompounded with any greed, hate, and delusion; that is, it is free from the three unskilful roots of action. It is the state free of all reactive tendencies. Unconditioned by any reactivity, it is the purely creative mind. Lest you think that this sounds just like you on a particularly good day, the Buddha also described nirvana in more demanding terms. For instance, it is imagined as a state of perfect calm and clarity:

> Just as . . . in the midst of mountains there was a lake whose water was clear, transparent and undisturbed, so standing on the bank someone with eyes might see oysters and shells, gravel and stones, and shoals of fish on the move or stationary.[34]

Moreover, it is a state into which an awakened person plunges; it is like the ocean into which all rivers flow, and into which someone who has entered the stream of the Dharma is carried.

The term 'unconditioned' should therefore be understood as part of a repertoire of ideas and images by which the Buddha tried to express the inexpressible, and this is probably the spirit in which to read the Buddha's famous metaphysical declaration:

> There is, monks, an unborn, an unbecome, an unmade, an unconditioned. If there were not an unborn, an unbecome, an unmade, an unconditioned, no escape could be discerned from what is born, become, made, and conditioned. But, monks, since there is an unborn, an unbecome, an unmade, an unconditioned, an escape can be discerned from what is born, become, made, and conditioned.[35]

Certainly there is no scope whatever for reading into this passage the existence of a transcendental 'ground of being', like the *Brahman* of the Upaniṣads, or the impersonal God of some forms of theology. The unconditioned existence taught by the Buddha is at once more mysterious and more practical than the goal of abstract metaphysics. It means human existence without the familiar conditions that keep us revolving in *dukkha*.

Questions for Chapter Seven

1. To what extent do you notice that your experience is constantly changing? Do you tend to notice more the arising or the passing away of what you experience? Is this different for pleasant and unpleasant experiences?
2. The Scottish philosopher, David Hume (1711–76), is known for a 'bundle theory' of the self that is very similar to the teaching of Buddhism:

   > When I enter most intimately into what I call myself, I always stumble on some particular perception or other, of heat or cold, light or shade, love or hatred, pain or pleasure. I never can catch myself at any time without a perception, and never can observe any thing but the perception. When my perceptions are removed for any time, as by sound sleep, so long am I insensible of myself, and may truly be said not to exist. And were all my perceptions removed by death, and could I neither think, nor feel, nor see, nor love, nor hate after the dissolution of my body, I should be entirely annihilated, nor do I conceive what is farther requisite to make me a perfect non-entity … man is a bundle or collection of different perceptions which succeed one another with an inconceivable rapidity and are in perpetual flux and movement.[36]

   Do you agree with David Hume? When you look into your experience, what do you find?
3. Try observing your own mind thinking. Is it possible to observe thoughts arising, and leading to other thoughts through a process of association? Is this process conscious, or unconscious, or something else? Is it you thinking, or is thinking just happening of its own accord?

Chapter Eight

Emptiness and Interdependence

To conclude this study of conditionality we will look beyond the Buddha's teaching, to some implications and interpretations of *paṭicca-samuppāda*. Our first topic will be that of *śūnyatā* or 'emptiness', a term equivalent to conditionality, as explained by the second-century-CE Indian philosopher Nāgārjuna. Our second will be the idea of the 'mutual interpenetration' of all things, developed by the Hua-yen school, established around the seventh century CE in China, and I will also discuss some English poetry that evokes the same vision of interconnectedness. Finally, we will explore conditionality as 'interdependence', which brings conditionality into conversation with themes in modern science.

Conditionality as 'emptiness'

Buddhism, like everything else, is subject to change. After his passing away, the Buddha's teachings were collected and preserved, first orally by monks who memorized and chanted them, and later in the form of written scriptures. Even while some Buddhists remembered and studied the words of the Buddha, others developed a philosophical interpretation of the teachings, known as 'Abhidharma'. We saw in Chapter Three how followers of Abhidharma developed, for instance, the three-life interpretation of the twelve *nidānas*: these thinkers were systematic and scholastic, seeking patterns and relationships, and they made their analyses of mind and mental events for the sake of cultivating skilful states. Their method involved analysing

technical terms in Buddhism

śūnyatā

(in Sanskrit; in Pali *suññata*), 'emptiness', derives from *śūnya*, 'empty', with the abstract suffix *-tā*, and signifies the absence of *svabhāva* or 'intrinsic existence' in all *dharmas*. Things are *śūnya* not in the sense of an empty bucket (containing nothing) but as in an empty forest (uninhabited and wild). 'Emptiness' should not be mistaken for 'non-existence'; 'insubstantiality' and 'voidness' are other possible translations that might have a less nihilistic resonance for some people. Most importantly, the concept of *śūnyatā* is itself empty, void, and without substantiality, just like everything else: the function of the idea is to point to the ultimate nature of reality without itself getting in the way.

---

experience into dharmas (or 'things') – distinct components of reality that could not be further analysed, such as the physical 'elements' of earth, water, fire, and air – and psychological 'events' such as feeling, attention, and greed. However, while this analysis makes sense as a method of analysing reality for the sake of spiritual practice, some Abhidharma thinkers decided that these dharmas really existed – despite the fact that the Buddha had taught that things are dependently arisen, and hence they neither really exist nor are completely non-existent.[1] The problem with such an analysis, if it is taken too literally, is that it locks up the dynamic, process-oriented, practical approach of the Buddha's teaching in an abstract intellectualism.

There was soon a reaction within the Buddhist tradition to the Abhidharma approach, in the form of the *Prajñāpāramitā* or 'Perfection of Wisdom' literature, which taught the *śūnyatā* or 'emptiness' of dharmas.[2] Then in the second century CE came Nāgārjuna, who used the concept of *śūnyatā* in order to counter the view that dharmas really exist, and to bring Buddhism back to the 'middle way' taught by the Buddha. The idea of *śūnyatā* is a philosophical development of the principle of conditionality. It follows from the principle of conditionality in that, if everything arises dependent on specific conditions, nothing can exist independently, from its own side, as it were, and hence everything is 'empty' (*śūnya*) of an independent essence. So to realize emptiness is to see the play of processes that constitute reality. For Nāgārjuna, *śūnyatā* is a vision of reality, a direct seeing that nothing has *svabhāva*, intrinsic existence, but that all things arise dependent on conditions. The point of spiritual practice is not to analyse experience into supposedly real elements, or dharmas, as the Abhidharmikas thought, but to directly know and see the impermanent, dependently arisen nature of things. For Nāgārjuna, *śūnyatā* was synonymous with conditionality:

> We claim that dependent arising (*pratītya-samutpāda*) is
> emptiness (*śūnyatā*),
> Which notion, once acquired, is truly the middle way.[3]

> Since there does not exist anything which is not
> dependently arisen,
> So there does not exist anything that is not empty.[4]

Nāgārjuna would have agreed with the Abhidharmikas that a tree, for instance, does not ultimately exist, but is dependently arisen, and made of dharmas such as earth, water, fire and air. Similarly, he would have agreed that human beings do not really exist as independent persons, but are constituted from the five *khandhas*. However, Nāgārjuna's equation of dependent arising with emptiness means that even these dharmas – the four elements and the five constituents – are empty, having no more intrinsic existence than trees and persons. It's emptiness all the way down. In practice this means that the Abhidharma analysis of mind and mental events is a useful tool, but the dharmas it describes do not really exist.

Even in Nāgārjuna's day, however, people could not help thinking that emptiness meant non-existence, and that his *mādhyamaka* ('middle way') meant nihilism – that nothing really existed, so nothing mattered. Most people are like Vacchagotta, who thought *anattā* meant he did not exist. Nāgārjuna's rebuttal of such misunderstandings was firm:

When viewed wrongly by those of weak intelligence,
emptiness is disastrous,
Like a snake handled wrongly, or a wrongly prepared
spell.[5]

Whether or not Nāgārjuna really believed in spells, he believed that those who saw his philosophy as nihilism were grasping the idea of *śūnyatā* wrongly. The middle way does not mean that things do not exist. The problem, he says, comes from confusing conventional (*saṃvṛti*) and ultimate (*paramārtha*) levels of truth:

The Dharma-teaching of the Buddhas is based on two
truths (*satya*):
The conventional truth of the world and that which is
ultimate.

Those who do not understand the distinction between
these two truths
Do not understand the truth (*tattva*) there is in Buddhist
doctrine.[6]

The two levels of truth give us a way to handle the concept of emptiness in the right way. From the conventional point of view, it is true that things exist as dependently arisen: they arise, they remain, and they pass away again. We talk about things as if they exist because it is useful and practical to do so, and the Buddha himself talked of 'you' and 'me', of 'trees' and 'persons', in accordance with the conventions of communication. But from the ultimate point of view there are no intrinsic existences behind the processes of arising and ceasing; there is just the flow of phenomena, and 'things' do not really arise or cease.

From Nāgārjuna's point of view, all this was simply a restatement of the original meaning of the Buddha's teaching, though with a bit more philosophical clarity. For instance, in one discourse the Buddha explains how the world is 'empty':

The venerable Ānanda approached the Blessed One, sat to one side, and while sitting said this to the Blessed One:

> 'Lord, it is said that "the world is empty, the world is empty". What does it mean, lord, to say "the world is empty (*suñña*)"?'
>
> 'Ānanda, it is because it is empty of the self or anything to do with the self that it is said that "the world is empty" ...'

The 'emptiness' of the world signifies the fact that no 'self' can be found anywhere in it. However, this only seems to make sense if we take it as a statement of ultimate truth. After all, on the conventional level the world is not empty and is full of people who believe they exist as a 'self'. What the Buddha means by 'world' is the world of experience, when this 'world' is analysed very closely in accordance with the Dharma:

> And what is empty of a self or anything to do with the self? The eye, Ānanda, is empty of a self or anything to do with the self. Form is empty of a self or anything to do with the self. Eye-consciousness is empty of a self or anything to do with the self. Eye-contact is empty of a self or anything to do with the self. Whatever arises with eye-contact as its condition, to be felt as pleasant, painful or neither, that is empty of a self or anything to do with the self. The ear is empty of a self or anything to do with the self ... The nose ... The tongue ... The body ... The mind ... Whatever arises with mind-contact as its condition, to be felt as pleasant, painful or neither, that is empty of a self or anything to do with the self.
>
> Ānanda, it is because it is empty of the self or anything to do with the self that it is said that 'the world is empty'.[7]

By 'world' the Buddha therefore means the world seen for what it really is – which is what Nāgārjuna calls the 'ultimate truth'. Elsewhere, the Buddha says that the constituents (*khandhas*) of experience are insubstantial – form is like froth, feelings are like bubbles, perceptions are like mirages, formations are like the soft pulp inside a banana tree, and consciousness is like a magical trick; and this insubstantiality of things appears when one looks at, reflects on and wisely examines experience.[8]

On the conventional level, of course, we may have families, jobs, and bills to pay. But holding the idea of *śūnyatā* in the right way, as ultimate truth, we can know that even *dukkha*, ignorance, craving, and so on are dependently arisen, without any intrinsic existence. We practise in order to realize this truth and to live from it. We are clear about what we are doing, where the spiritual life is heading, and we do not mistake the passing world, least of all our own thoughts and feelings, for ultimate reality.

Perhaps the word 'emptiness' is not the most encouraging of words to describe the ultimate truth. The scholar Herbert Guenther preferred to translate *śūnyatā* as 'openness', or even as 'the open dimension of being'.[9] Such an interpretation of a technical term is a more positive reminder of the mysterious nature of reality. In this sense, Nāgārjuna's philosophy of *śūnyatā* returns us to our description (in Chapter One) of *paṭicca-samuppāda* as a 'transcendental principle', a form of words that points to a reality beyond words and concepts.

Mutual interpenetration

With the concept of emptiness we have entered deeply into the world of Buddhist metaphysics, that is, ideas about ultimate reality – despite all of the Buddha's misgivings about metaphysical thinking, and the very practical emphasis of *paṭicca-samuppāda*. Nāgārjuna's philosophy of *śūnyatā*, however, is carefully formulated to leave us with nothing to hang on to, since the emptiness of reality means 'empty of all concepts' – so, rather than being an irrelevant speculative idea, emptiness takes us to the heart of the Dharma. It points to the inexpressible nature of things, in just the way that *paṭicca-samuppāda* does. Certain poets and mystics, however, have been dissatisfied with the purely apophatic approach of only saying what reality, since it is ultimately inexpressible, is not. In Buddhism, it is in the Mahāyāna tradition that we find positive metaphysical accounts of the nature of reality. Here I will mention just one example of such metaphysics – that of the complete mutual interpenetration of all things, as taught in the Hua-yen school.

The Hua-yen (or 'Flower Garland') school flourished in China from the sixth to the ninth century CE.[10] Its vision of reality is a systematization of that found in the *Avataṃsaka Sūtra*, the Mahāyāna scripture after which it is named. This enormous *sūtra* uses mind-expanding ideas and images to evoke how reality appears to a Buddha, and it culminates with a mystical vision of the Buddha Vairocana's tower, which, Tardis-like, contains innumerable other towers, each with a Buddha teaching the Dharma, and with every tower perfectly visible and none obstructing any other.[11] This is a visionary and poetic extrapolation of *śūnyatā*: if everything is empty of intrinsic existence, then everything depends on everything else and in a sense contains everything else. The Hua-yen thinkers developed this vision in terms of the mutual interpenetration of everything. The universe is imagined as a wondrous net of jewels, in which each jewel reflects every other jewel in an infinite play of light. The Hua-yen Buddhist scholar Francis Cook evokes this vision attractively:

> Far away in the heavenly abode of the great god Indra, there is a wonderful net which has been hung by some cunning artificer in such a manner that it stretches out indefinitely in all directions. In accordance with the extravagant tastes of deities, the artificer has hung a single glittering jewel at each 'eye' of the net, and since the net is infinite in dimension, the jewels are infinite in number. There hang the jewels, glittering like stars of the first magnitude, a wonderful sight to behold. If we now arbitrarily select one of these jewels for inspection and look closely at it, we will discover that in its polished surface there are reflected *all* the other jewels in the net, infinite in number. Not only that, but each of the jewels reflected in this one jewel is also reflecting all the other jewels, so that there is an infinite reflecting process occurring.[12]

To see reality in this way – as a vast net of dependently arisen phenomena, each showing the influence of everything else – is to see the world as an awakened being sees it, so mutual interpenetration is an expression of ultimate rather than conventional truth. In Hua-yen terms, it is the nature of the *dharmadhātu*, the 'realm of reality' inhabited by Buddhas.

For many, this may sound like a wonderfully inspiring vision of reality. However, some Buddhists have criticized the idea of mutual interpenetration because it brings metaphysical theory into Buddhism.[13] According to such critics, the idea of mutual interpenetration implies 'simultaneous mutual arising', which means that things arise together, all dependent upon one another, all at the same time. Because of simultaneous mutual arising, there is mutual identity – ultimately everything is one undifferentiated totality. If *śūnyatā* means an undifferentiated totality, then it has become a word for the underlying reality of the universe, and such a metaphysical theory is not part of the Buddha's teaching. However, if we consider mutual interpenetration as an expression of ultimate truth rather than a theory about the metaphysical nature of ordinary reality, there might be no problem. We might nevertheless wish to bear in mind that mutual interpenetration is a peculiarly Chinese contribution to Buddhist thought, reflecting the assimilation of Taoist ideas into Buddhism.

The 'poetry of interconnectedness'

We would be wise, therefore, to regard the idea of mutual interpenetration as a Chinese poetic vision of the nature of reality rather than as philosophy, and in this sense it bears some comparison with similar attempts by European poets to evoke the nature of things in metaphysical terms. It might be useful to explore a little of such poetry (since it is framed in thought-forms probably more familiar in the west than Chinese ones) so that we might begin to make our own connections with how reality appears to a Buddha. In earlier chapters we had William Blake's 'world in a grain of sand' and Wordsworth's 'sense sublime / of something... deeply interfused'. Such poets wished to express how everything in the universe is joined together in one overarching natural order. Here is the English poet Alexander Pope's version of this vision of reality:

> Look round our world; behold the chain of love
> Combining all below and all above.
> See plastic Nature working to this end,
> The single atoms each to other tend,
> Attract, attracted to, the next in place
> Formed and impelled its neighbour to embrace.
> See matter next, with various life endued,
> Press to one centre still, the general good:
> See dying vegetables life sustain,
> See life dissolving vegetate again:
> All forms that perish other forms supply
> (By turns we catch the vital breath, and die),
> Like bubbles on the sea of matter borne,
> They rise, they break, and to that sea return.
> Nothing is foreign; parts relate to whole;
> One all-extending, all-preserving soul
> Connects each being, greatest with the least,
> Made beast in aid of man, and man of beast;
> All served, all serving; nothing stands alone;
> The chain holds on, and where it ends unknown.[14]

In Pope's eighteenth-century vision, the medieval idea of a 'Great Chain of Being', linking God to all beings in a hierarchy, has given way (under the influence of the natural sciences) to a less hierarchical vision of an interconnected universe, with 'one soul' underlying the connected parts of the whole of nature. This optimistic philosophy of nature can to some degree replace belief in God, as it now seems that humanity has a place in a meaningful cosmos. There is a clear echo here of the way in which the Buddha's teaching of *paṭicca-samuppāda* seeks to explain the nature of things without resorting either to a creator (God or Brahmā) or to saying that existence is random and meaningless.

The nineteenth-century Romantic poets further developed this vision of nature into a pantheistic, pagan faith in the 'One

Life' that runs through all things. Many of the Romantics sought, through poetry and art (and love), to rediscover a sense of the oneness in things. These lines by the English poet Samuel Taylor Coleridge express the mood:

> O! the one Life within us and abroad,
> Which meets all motions and becomes its soul,
> A light in sound, a sound-like power in light,
> Rhythm in all thought, and joyance every where –
> Methinks, it should have been impossible
> Not to love all things in a world so fill'd;
> Where the breeze warbles, and the mute still air
> Is music slumbering on her instrument.[15]

These lines are as much about the nature of the mind as about the external world. According to Coleridge's thought, based on the revolutionary philosophy of Immanuel Kant, our perception of things outside us is not a passive reception of sensory information but an active participation in a process that involves external forms and our senses as well as the mind's powers of recognition and imagination. To recognize the 'One Life' is therefore to recognize how our experienced reality is to a large degree the product of the creative imagination, which recognizes itself when it feels the underlying unity of all experienced things. These ideas bear comparison with the Mind-Only school of Buddhist philosophy. Again, we do not have to take this 'poetry of interconnectedness' as philosophical metaphysics. It is more of a heart-felt vision. And just as Hua-yen thought is particularly Chinese, so the Romantic conception of nature as a living and interconnected whole might be particularly relevant to modern westerners, as it offers a more wholesome alternative to the predominant mechanistic world view. Such poetry is perhaps a gateway for people seeking to engage more fully with the Buddha's teaching of conditionality from our Western cultural perspective.[16]

Interdependence and conditionality

The themes discussed so far in this chapter – emptiness, mutual interpenetration and interconnectedness – concern the ultimate reality of things. The theme of interdependence, however, is more down to earth and practical, as it is simply another way of thinking about conditionality. If all things are dependently arisen, they depend on everything else, both for their arising and for their continued existence. In this sense things are interdependent. Sangharakshita reflects on interdependence like this:

> Causality is a complex web; anything that happens or comes into being does so as a result not of one cause, but of many. Indeed – and this is an aspect of the Buddha's insight into reality – if one reflects on the factors that have produced the coming together of any phenomenon, there is simply no end to them. Consider, for example, what has 'caused' the loaf of bread (or the bag of rice) in your kitchen. Think of the people involved – and what 'caused' them. Think of their ancestry, stretching into beginningless time. Think of the sun and the rain and the earth; think of the transportation and packaging materials. Really, there is nothing, and no one, who has not been involved in the coming into being – and into your kitchen – of that loaf of bread. This is, incidentally, another way of coming at the truth of *anātman*, 'no separate selfhood'. Reflection shows us that nothing has an 'own-being' separate from everything else; everything and everyone is interconnected.[17]

We can use the concept of interdependence in this sense to reflect on how our own lives are bound up with others, and how the sense of being a separate self or ego tends to obscure that truth. Next time you sit down for dinner you could spend a moment reflecting, before you eat, on where all the various parts of your meal come from. Each has been produced by people somewhere, transported by people, prepared by people. Many people have invested their time and effort in order that you can now eat. Your dinner depends on so many conditions.[18]

On this everyday level, interdependence means the way particular things depend on particular conditions. It does not mean that everything is interdependent with everything else – my cornflakes with my coffee, your mood with the postman's – only that particular things depend on quite *specific* conditions. At any moment we can reflect on some of the specific conditions upon which any particular thing depends. In this everyday sense, interdependence is not as general and mystical a vision as the complete mutual interpenetration of all phenomena in the Hua-yen tradition. Perhaps ultimately it is true that everything is connected to everything else in the universe, but in this ultimate sense everything is also empty and inexpressible.

Thinking about conditionality as interdependence also brings us into a useful dialogue with ecology. The American scholar and activist Joanna Macy has written on the relationship between dependent arising and contemporary systems theory, in such a way as to bring the teaching of conditionality into conversation with contemporary ecological conceptions of interdependence. Her exploration of *paṭicca-samuppāda* in relation to systems theory opens up a valuable way into appreciating the nature of the Buddha's teaching.[19]

When we first encounter *paṭicca-samuppāda* we are likely to relate to it in terms of causality, under the influence of the long sweep of western philosophy and science. In the classical scientific paradigm of how change takes place, a cause produces an effect in a one-way direction: the moon causes the tides, viruses cause us to catch colds, beautiful music causes joy. This paradigm has been very successful for accurately explaining the workings of nature. Scientists have succeeded in discovering mathematical laws that describe the patterns found in the natural world in terms of cause and effect. The success of the one-way linear causal paradigm has led to the general assumption that it is the way the world works.

However, this is partly an illusion created by always assuming that we can explain situations by finding one-way causal influences at work. As Macy remarks:

> This methodology has yielded powerful results. They seem, at least until recently, to have served the goals of analysis, predictability and control. But, as the tools and inquiries of scientists expand, it is increasingly evident that the universe does not always conform to expectations. When events interact and patterns are superimposed on each other, they yield novel, unpredictable, nonlinear results.[20]

What this means is that scientists in the past tended to see linear causation everywhere because they were not looking for anything else. But recent work in quantum physics and in mathematical chaos theory, for instance, has opened up different ways of looking at the world.[21] We are in fact surrounded by non-linear systems of causal interaction where the laws that can be discerned do not yield simple, predictable results. Weather patterns are one example, and another is the ripples in sand on the seashore, left behind by the retreating tide. The patterns of ripples are not caused directly by the water or directly by the sand; they emerge from processes of interaction between water and sand resulting in unpredictable complex structures within certain limits.

This study of conditionality has mainly been devoted to explaining the Buddha's teaching of conditionality as it is found in the early Buddhist texts. This teaching is primarily concerned with human experience, and the conditions upon which both *dukkha* and liberation arise. Now, if our modern conceptions of interdependence and non-linear processes bear some comparison with the Buddha's conception of dependent arising, then we might be able to describe human experience not only as dependently arisen but also as an interdependent non-linear system. Indeed, I think that using these concepts helps bring the Buddha's teaching to life in modern western terms.

In Chapter One we considered the experience of stress, and how the factors that give rise to it interact in complex ways. For

Figure 5: *Sand ripples form from the unpredictable, non-linear interplay of sand and tide.*

instance, insomnia can increase stress, and stress can increase insomnia. This is an example of something that arises on conditions, but not in a linear way. Stress is a complex phenomenon interdependent on several factors. Recognizing this allows us to investigate our experience with greater sensitivity to its complex nature. Perhaps much of our suffering comes from not understanding how complex the world is, and how many factors are involved in our experience. Generally speaking, for instance, human beings do not understand the nature of happiness. Many surveys show that an increase in wealth has little effect on our happiness above a certain amount needed for a financially secure life. Yet many people strive hard to obtain more money, and our countries' economies are geared to increase GDP in the belief that increased financial prosperity is linked to an increase in well-being.[22]

Joanna Macy's suggestion is that the Buddha's teaching of conditionality involves interdependence and complex mutual arising rather than linear causality.[23] As we know, the Buddha was concerned primarily with *dukkha*, its arising and ceasing. While the twelve links of dependent arising *look* like a linear sequence, they have to be understood as a complex interacting system, each factor contributing to the arising of *dukkha* as well as involved in complex interactions with other factors. This is particularly evident in certain versions of the chain of dependent arising. Some begin with the reciprocal dependence of consciousness (*viññāṇa*) and name-and-form (*nāma-rūpa*), in a system of mutual arising.[24] A complex process is also evident in a very common way wherein the Buddha explains the process of perception:

> And what, monks, is the origin of *dukkha*? Dependent on the eye (or ear, nose, tongue, body, or mind) and forms (or sounds, odours, tastes, touchables, or thoughts) arises visual (or auditory, olfactory, gustatory, bodily, or mental) consciousness. The coming together of the three is contact. With contact as condition there is feeling. With feeling as condition there is craving. This, monks, is the origin of *dukkha*.[25]

In formulations of conditionality like this, the Buddha emphasized the complex interactions involved in experience. We should therefore understand the twelve *nidānas* as representing a dynamic, interrelated system that, through ignorance and craving, produces *dukkha*. I am not suggesting that the twelve *nidānas* are all completely interdependent, only that the way that they are presented by the Buddha should not be taken literally to represent a one-way linear causal process. The specific conditions on which the *nidānas* arise are complex and interdependent. We can also see specific interdependent arising at work in presentations of the path. In Chapter 4 we explored three different ways in which the Buddha taught the arising of the spiritual path: from *dukkha* and faith; from ethics; and from wise attention. Thinking about the path as an interdependent dynamic system, we might say that these three entrances to the path condition and support one another, and the joy (*pāmojja*) that arises from our efforts is a product of several different conditions.

Interdependence, therefore, when understood in terms of the non-linear causal paradigm of systems theory, offers a useful way for modern westerners to approach the Buddha's practical teaching of conditionality. This teaching is a key to unlock the mysteries of life – a key to be used in our actual lives and situations, which all arise on conditions. The mysteries may be deep and profound, but the teaching of conditionality remains the Buddha's great gift to us.

Questions for Chapter Eight

1. What might it mean to see your thoughts and emotions as *śūnya*, empty? How would that affect your relationship to them? How might you come to see them more as 'empty' in this way?
2. Let us explore ways in which seeing interdependence might be useful. In what ways might it be helpful to realize how you are dependent on others? In what ways might it be helpful to realize your influence on others? How might you encourage yourself to realize interdependence in these helpful ways?
3. Miguel is the ten-year-old son of a small-scale independent coffee grower in a poor South American country, and he would like to work with computers when he grows up. Thinking about interconnectedness in a practical sense, what is our connection with Miguel, and what might be our ethical responsibilities towards him?

Appendix

24 *Nidāna* Reflection

Introductory note

The following guided reflection is designed to support contemplation of the Buddha's teaching of *paṭicca-samuppāda* as a means of gaining liberating insight into the human situation. The guided reflection provides an opportunity to investigate in your own experience the series of twelve *nidānas* describing samsara that lead to *dukkha,* and the twelve positive *nidānas* that lead to awakening.[1]

The 24 *nidāna* reflection was originally devised by Sangharakshita. The more traditional contemplation of the twelve cyclic *nidānas* begins with contemplation of ignorance, *avijjā,* and so on, up to ageing-and-death, *jarā-maraṇa,* followed by a contemplation of those same *nidānas* as they cease. Sangharakshita extended this traditional contemplation by embedding it within a contemplation of the series of twelve positive *nidānas* describing the path to awakening, starting with *dukkha* and faith, *saddhā.* The 24 *nidāna* reflection described below is a simplified version of that devised by Sangharakshita. In it, the twelve cyclic *nidānas* are contemplated in a single series as both arising and ceasing. This slight simplification is intended to make the reflection more manageable for meditators new to such a practice.[2]

A reflection practice like the 24 *nidāna* reflection offers an opportunity to allow profound teachings like that of conditionality to sink in at the emotional and existential level, so that it takes on a meaning beyond that of doctrine and thought. Reflection in this sense may not be a matter of thinking so much as a quiet abiding with certain ideas, in order to find a deeper response to them. A method of practice is therefore simply to keep attention in the heart area as you read or hear the following topics for reflection, and to allow ideas, feelings and associations to arise. You could think of this practice as being like dropping stones into a well while looking and listening for what happens as they disappear into the darkness. In this way, the teachings on conditionality will find their way into your being at a more profound level, and can inform your life accordingly.

For those who may wish to incorporate the 24 *nidāna* reflection into an existing meditation practice, I offer the following advice: It is quite possible to include the reflection in a regular meditation session. However, you might find that it works better if it is done after a short period of calming (*samatha*) meditation, such as the mindfulness of breathing or the cultivation of loving-kindness (*mettā-bhāvanā*). It is also advisable to spend some time after the reflection just sitting, in order to allow the practice to sink in. The more concentrated one's mind is to begin with, the deeper the reflection can go. You may therefore find that the 24 *nidāna* practice is particularly suitable for retreats, since the retreat situation is more likely to provide the calm and quiet conducive to effective reflection.

Part 1: the spiral path

In preparation for this period of reflection I recommend that you take up a comfortable posture in which you know that your body will be comfortable for about 45 minutes. This might be on a meditation cushion or stool, or it might be on a firm chair. It is important to spend some time before the reflection allowing the mind to settle, and bringing awareness into the body.

1. We begin our reflection by bringing to mind *dukkha*, suffering, unsatisfactoriness, pain, difficulty, the fact that life can be a rough ride. The Buddha's first noble truth is that *there is dukkha*. This *dukkha* is felt in the body as pain and in the mind as difficulty and dissatisfaction. It hasn't

arisen to spite us, and it will not go away because we don't like it. It simply arises on conditions and ceases when those conditions cease.

2. Out of this experience of *dukkha* can arise *saddhā*: faith, trust, and confidence that we can give rise to a path of life and practice that will lead beyond *dukkha*. This faith might be emotional – heartfelt devotion; it might be intellectual – clear appreciation; it might be volitional – strong determination.
3. When one has discovered faith, then joy, *pāmojja*, will arise. This joy is the gladness, hope, and optimism that arises from an experience of faith and of the Buddhist path. It also arises through ethical practice. Keeping the precepts leads to freedom from remorse, and this too leads to the joy of a clear conscience and of being a positive presence in the world. Joy also arises from paying mindful attention to our experience, so that the reactive mind is not the dominant force in operation.
4. As this joy becomes more natural to us we may begin to experience rapture, *pīti*. This rapture is the physical thrill of life-energy releasing through us as we meditate with commitment, or as we act with integrity, or as we immerse ourselves in the inspiring beauty of nature, or of art, or of friendship.
5. With rapture as condition arises tranquillity, *passaddhi*. As the physical thrill of rapture dies down we enjoy the integrated exhilaration of continued physical and mental pleasure. Our bodies relax and our minds enjoy a calm tranquillity.
6. Out of this tranquillity arises bliss, *sukha*. This bliss is the underlying sense of well-being that results from practising the Buddhist path. It can endure even through life's ups and downs. It is not necessarily something felt but may be a happiness that is independent of how life feels.
7. This bliss is the condition on which arises concentration, *samādhi*. This concentration is the steady mental attention we can bring to our experience when we are fully

integrated and aware. It is an undistracted succession of positive mental events.

8. When there is concentration there can be knowledge and vision of reality, *yathā-bhūta-ñāṇa-dassana*. Through steady, concentrated attention arises insight-knowledge, seen with the eye of the heart. We know that all that arises passes away, and we no longer seek satisfaction in what is bound to disappoint us.

Part 2: the cyclic *nidānas*

Having contemplated the first half of the spiral path we turn to the twelve *nidānas* of samsara in order to reflect on the conditions by which *dukkha* has come into existence, the cessation of which brings the end of suffering.

1. The twelve *nidānas* begin with ignorance, *avijjā*. This spiritual ignorance is the basic condition of our avoidable suffering. It means not knowing and understanding which actions of body, speech, and mind lead to *dukkha*. It implies a commitment to a separate and enduring personality. But it is not our true nature. With the cessation of the defiling emotions of greed, hate, and delusion, and with the attainment of liberating insight, ignorance will cease.
2. With ignorance as condition arise the formations, or *saṅkhāras*. When there is spiritual ignorance, there arise habitual actions, ways of speech, and patterns of thought that lead to *dukkha*. We did not create these reactive formations, but they cause us to suffer. But neither are we obliged to live according to reactive formations. If ignorance was to cease, formations would dissolve into liberating creative awareness.
3. With the formations as condition arises consciousness, *viññāṇa*. When there is ignorance and there are reactive habitual formations, there arises a self-consciousness of being different and separate from the world we live

in. If formations were to cease, consciousness would be liberated from limiting views.

4. With consciousness as condition arises name-and-form, *nāma-rūpa*. When there is consciousness of being a separate self, there arises the manifest world of material forms and mental ideas that seem to exist apart from the perceiver. If there were a cessation of dualistic consciousness, the world of name-and-form would be seen for what it is.
5. Dependent on name-and-form arise the six sense realms, the *saḷāyātanāni*. When there is a manifest world seeming to exist apart from the perceiver, the world of sense-experience springs into existence. If the world of name-and-form was seen for what it is, the six sense realms would be understood.
6. Dependent on the six sense realms arises contact, *phassa*. When there is a world of sense-experience, there can be contact between the perceiver and an object perceived. If the six sense realms were understood, the nature of the contact between a self and a world would be seen for what it is.
7. With contact as condition arises feeling, *vedanā*. When there is contact between a perceiver and particular objects in the world, there arises the experience of 'this is pleasant', 'this is unpleasant', and 'this is neither', in what is seen, heard, tasted, smelled, touched, and thought. If there were no contact – if the sense-gates were well guarded – then pleasant, unpleasant, and neutral feelings would not arise.
8. Dependent on feeling arises craving, *taṇhā*. When there is the experience of 'this is pleasant', 'this is unpleasant' and 'this is neither', there arises craving, aversion, and confusion in one whose experience is based on ignorance and habitual formations. This is the burning fire of *dukkha*, of unsatisfied desire. But if there is mindful awareness around feelings, then craving, aversion, and confusion will not necessarily arise.
9. Dependent on craving arises clinging, *upādāna*, which we can also translate as grasping. When there is craving,

aversion, and confusion, there is clinging to sense-pleasures, clinging to views, clinging to modes of conduct and ways of life, and clinging to a fixed sense of self. If there were no craving, aversion, and confusion, there would be no need for this clinging that sustains *dukkha*.

10. Dependent on clinging arises existence or becoming, *bhava*. When there is clinging that sustains *dukkha*, then there is the condition for renewed existence in samsara, that is, for re-becoming in the six realms with their various kinds of experience. If there were no clinging or grasping, then there would be no existence or re-becoming anywhere.
11. With existence as condition there is birth, *jāti*. When there is existence and re-becoming in samsara, then there is coming into being, new existence, the arising of a new experience with a new sense of self. If there were no re-becoming in samsara then there would be no new birth and coming into being.
12. When there is birth, there is ageing-and-death, *jarā-maraṇa*. When there is birth, new existence, new experience, then there is the ageing, decay, falling apart, disintegration, and death of what has come into existence. If there were no birth then there could be no ageing-and-death. Thus has arisen this whole mass of *dukkha*; and thus, with the cessation of its conditions, this whole mass of *dukkha* can cease.

Part 3: the spiral path (concluded)

Having contemplated the arising and the ceasing of *dukkha* through reflecting on the twelve cyclic *nidānas*, we can complete our contemplation of the spiral path:

9. With the arising of knowledge and vision of reality there can then arise disenchantment, *nibbidā*. Seeing how *dukkha* has arisen through spiritual ignorance, through craving and clinging, we are disinclined to continue with it. The spell of samsara has been broken. Instead of holding

out for future satisfaction we prefer to live with mindful awareness of what is.

10. And with the arising of disenchantment arises dispassion, *virāga*. Living with insight into the arising of *dukkha*, we are no longer emotionally caught up in what used to enchant us. If we were disenchanted and dispassionate, we would be free to enjoy life without obsession and to extend our *mettā* and compassion more effectively.
11. With the arising of dispassion arises liberation, *vimutti*. When we are no longer emotionally involved in the world of *dukkha*, we are liberated from it. We are released from the obligation to suffer. Whatever experience comes our way we no are no longer inclined to react, but bring creative responses to whatever arises.
12. Finally, with liberation as condition arises knowledge of the destruction of the pollutants. With liberation comes the knowledge that one is liberated, and that the forces and tendencies that used to dominate experience are no longer there. This is synonymous with *arahant*-ship, awakening, Buddhahood.

To conclude this period of reflection I recommend you spend some time sitting quietly, allowing your experience of contemplation to fully sink in.

Concluding note:

The reflections on the *nidānas* given here are merely suggestions of, and indications towards, the truths involved. I recommend that, once you have accustomed yourself to the practice, you conduct your own investigations and studies into each of the links. That is, the reflections given above are not phrases to be memorized as if it were the words that were important, but signs pointing towards connections and insights you have to make for yourself. Your exploration will then be in the spirit of the Buddha's 'three levels of understanding'. First there is the understanding that comes through *listening* or *learning* (*suta-mayā paññā*): you might reread sections of this book, or follow up some references, to make sure you have understood the meaning of each *nidāna*. Then there is the understanding that comes through *thinking* or *reflecting* (*cintā-mayā paññā*): you might spend time reflecting more specifically on individual links to clarify them in your mind. And third, there is the understanding that comes through *reflecting* or *cultivating* (*bhāvanā-mayā paññā*): having internalized a sense of what each *nidāna* means, you will be able to meditate on the 24 *nidānas* directly, turning your mind towards ideas now familiar and brimming with associations.[3]

Pronunciation Guide for Pali and Sanskrit Words

The pronunciation of Pali and Sanskrit words is completely regular and quite easy, once you know how to understand the diacritics used to mark particular sounds.[1]

The **vowels** are pronounced as in the following words:

a *as in* cut	**ā** *as in* cart
i *as in* kick	**ī** *as in* keep
u *as in* soot	**ū** *as in* suit
e *as in* hay	**ai** *as in* high
o *as in* oat	**au** *as in* out

The pronunciation of the semivowel **ṛ** is similar to the 'r' sound in words like 'trip' or 'pretty', but with some rolling of the sound.

The **consonants** correspond to their English equivalents, with the following qualifications:

g *as in* god **c** *as in* church **j** *as in* jay

ṭ and **ḍ** as English t and d, but with the tongue tip curled up and backwards against the roof of the mouth

t and **d** as English t and d, but with the tongue tip against the back of the upper front teeth

ś *and* **ṣ** *as in* sh

The **nasal sounds**, i.e. **ṅ**, **ñ**, **ṇ**, **n**, and **m**: before a consonant they make the natural spontaneous nasal sound associated with that consonant:

ṅk *as in* trunk **ṅg** *as in* sang

ñc *as in* crunch **ñj** *as in* binge

ṇṭ *or* **nt** *as in* tent, but with the above distinctions between ṭ and t

ṇḍ *or* **nd** *as in* bend, but with the above distinctions between ḍ and d

mp *as in* pimp **mb** *as in* bimbo

The anusvara, **ṃ** (sometimes written **ṁ**), is a pure nasal and can replace any of the above sounds. Before vowels:

ñ *as in* banyan

ṇ *and* **n** *as in* nit, but with the same distinction as between ṭ or ḍ and t and d

m *as in* mope

ṅ does not occur

The **aspirated consonants** are those which are shown followed immediately by the letter h, e.g. **gh**, **ch**, **th**, **ṭh** etc., and should be pronounced as indicated, but with an audible out-breath. Note that **th** is *not* pronounced as in 'there' or 'thick' but like the 'th' in hothouse, and **ph** is *not* pronounced as in 'pheasant' but like the 'ph' in mophead.

Doubled consonants are pronounced as such:

sadda as in sled-dog

the combination **kṣ** as in duck-shoot

The visarga, **ḥ**, is pronounced as a slight echo of the preceding vowel, or as an audible out-breath.

Glossary of Pali and Sanskrit Buddhist Terms

abhidhamma (Pali) = **abhidharma** (Sanskrit): the third division of the Buddhist scriptures (*tipiṭaka*, or 'three baskets'), the 'higher' or 'further teachings', concerned with the analysis of reality, especially mental states, into its elements (***dharmas***).

akusala (Pali) = **akuśala** (Sanskrit): unskilful; an action (***karma***) or mental state (***dharma***) is said to be ethically unskilful when rooted in greed (***lobha***), hate (***dosa***), or delusion (***moha***); unskilful states (***dharmas***) and actions (***karma***) do not conduce to meditative concentration (***samādhi***) or insight, and will have future unpleasant results (***vipākas***).

akusala-mūla (Pali) = **akuśala-mūla** (Sanskrit): unskilful root, three defilements (***kilesa***) that conduce to unskilful (***akusala***) actions (***karma***): (1) greed (***lobha***), (2) hate (***dosa***), and (3) delusion (***moha***).

anattā (Pali) = **anātman** (Sanskrit): not-self, the third characteristic (***lakkhaṇa***), as in *sabbe dhammā anattā*, 'all things are not-self', in the sense of being devoid of an ***ātman*** or unchanging self.

anicca (Pali) = **anitya** (Sanskrit): impermanent, the first characteristic (***lakkhaṇa***) as in *sabbe saṅkhārā aniccā*, 'all conditioned things are impermanent.'

aniccatā (Pali) = **anityatā** (Sanskrit): impermanence, the condition of being ***anitya***.

arahant (Pali) = **arhat** (Sanskrit): worthy one, someone who has realized full awakening; a term borrowed by the **Buddha** from the vocabulary of the ***samaṇas***.

ariya-saccāni (Pali) = **ārya-satyāni** (Sanskrit): noble truths or ennobling realities: (1) ***dukkha***, (2) the origin of ***dukkha*** (which is ***taṇhā***, craving), (3) the cessation of ***dukkha***, and (4) the path leading to the cessation of ***dukkha***.

asaṅkhata (Pali) = **asaṃskṛta** (Sanskrit): unconditioned, not arisen on conditions; an epithet of ***nirvāṇa***, which is permanent bliss (***sukha***).

Assaji (Pali) = **Aśvajit** (Sanskrit): one of a group of five monks who practised austerities with the Buddha-to-be, and later became his first disciples.

ātman (Sanskrit) = **attā** (Pali): self; the **Upaniṣads** taught the ***ātman*** as the metaphysical essence of the person, identical with ***Brahman***, denying which the **Buddha** taught ***anattā***.

avijjā (Pali) = **avidyā** (Sanskrit): ignorance; the spiritual ignorance which keeps us revolving in ***saṃsāra***; the first of the twelve ***nidānas***.

avyākata (Pali & Sanskrit): unanswered, as in the ten 'unanswered questions' about speculative metaphysics that the **Buddha** refused to answer because they are irrelevant.

bhava (Pali & Sanskrit): existence or becoming; the state of continuing existence in any realm of existence, and the tenth of the twelve ***nidānas***.

bhavacakra (Pali & Sanskrit): the wheel of existence or becoming, usually rendered 'Wheel of Life', the traditional Buddhist depiction of ***saṃsāra***.

bodhisatta (Pali) = **bodhisattva** (Sanskrit): a **Buddha** prior to his awakening, literally 'one-who-is-capable-of-awakening'.

bojjhaṅgas (Pali) = **bodhyaṅgas** (Sanskrit): the factors that lead to awakening, namely, (1) mindfulness (*sati*), (2) investigation of states (*dhammavicaya*), (3) energy (*viriya*), (4) rapture (***pīti***), (5) tranquillity (***passaddhi***), (6) concentration (***samādhi***), and (7) equanimity (*upekkhā*).

Brahman (Pali & Sanskrit): the underlying reality or truth taught in the **Upaniṣads**, with which the unchanging personal self or ***ātman*** is supposedly identical.

brahman (in Pali & Sanskrit: **brāhmaṇa**): a hereditary priest of the Vedic religion, a high-caste person; the **Buddha** also used the term in a positive sense to mean 'holy man'.

Buddha (Pali & Sanskrit): the awakened one, or more poetically the enlightened one, an epithet of Gotama, the founder of Buddhism, and for past and future teachers of awakening.

bodhi (Pali & Sanskrit): awakening, and, in a poetic sense, enlightenment.

cetanā (Pali & Sanskrit): intention or volition, what is done with the mind.

dharma (Sanskrit) = **dhamma** (Pali): (1) the teaching of the **Buddha** (the **Dharma**), to which a Buddhist goes for refuge; (2) the truth (also the **Dharma**); (3) the nature of reality (also the **Dharma**); (4) a state, mental state or simply a thing as an element of reality (a **dharma**).

dosa (Pali) = **dveṣa** (Sanskrit): hate, a defiling emotion (***kilesa***) and the second of the three unskilful roots (***akusala-mūla***).

dukkha (Pali) = **duḥkha** (Sanskrit): (1) painful, as in painful feeling (***vedanā***); and also (2) pain, suffering, unsatisfactoriness, discontent, life's being a rough ride: the **Dharma** begins with ***dukkha*** in ordinary human experience; the first noble truth (***āriya-sacca***) is that there is ***dukkha***; the first factor (***nidāna***) of the spiral path.

hetu (Pali & Sanskrit): cause or condition; *hetu* is synonymous with ***paccaya*** in early Buddhism but is later used to mean cause as distinct from ***paccaya***, meaning condition.

jarā-maraṇaṃ (Pali & Sanskrit): 'ageing and death', the last of the twelve ***nidānas***.

jāti (Pali & Sanskrit): birth, the eleventh of the twelve ***nidānas***.

jhāna (Pali) = **dhyāna** (Sanskrit): meditative absorption, included in ***samādhi***.

karma (Sanskrit) = **kamma** (Pali): intentional action, characterized as skilful (***kusala***) or unskilful (***akusala***), and having later consequences (***vipāka***) corresponding to its ethical quality.

khandhas (Pali) = **skandhas** (Sanskrit): the constituents of the person, the five aggregates or heaps: (1) form (***rūpa***), (2) feeling (***vedanā***), (3) perception (*saṭṭā*), (4) formations (***saṅkhāras***) and (5) consciousness (***viññāṇa***).

kilesa (Pali) = **kleśa** (Sanskrit): a defilement or affliction, such as the defiling emotions of greed (***lobha***), hate (***dveṣa***), and delusion (***moha***).

kusala (Pali) = **kuśala** (Sanskrit): skilful; an action (***kamma***) or mental state (***dharma***) is said to be ethically skilful when rooted in non-greed (***alobha***), non-hate (***adosa***) or non-delusion (***amoha***); skilful states (***dharmas***) and actions (***karma***) conduce to meditative concentration (***samādhi***) and insight, and will have future pleasant results (***vipākas***).

kusala-mūla (Pali) = **kuśala-mūla** (Sanskrit): skilful root, three states (***dharmas***) that conduce to skilful (***kusala***) actions (***karma***): (1) non-greed or contentment (***alobha***), (2) non-hate or love (***adosa***), and (3) non-delusion or wisdom (***amoha***).

lakkhaṇa (Pali) = **lakṣaṇa** (Sanskrit): a characteristic or mark, as in the three characteristics of the conditioned (***saṅkhata***): impermanence (***aniccatā***), unsatisfactoriness (***dukkhatā***), and being without a self (***anattātā***).

lobha (Pali & Sanskrit): greed, a defiling emotion (***kilesa***) and the first of the three unskilful roots (***akusala-mūla***).

Mahāyāna (Pali & Sanskrit): the Great Vehicle, a form of Buddhism that developed in India from the first century CE, later spreading to China, Tibet, Korea and Japan, with its own *sūtras* and schools, and teaching the '**bodhisattva** ideal' of attaining Buddhahood for the sake of all beings.

majjhimā paṭipadā (Pali) = **madhyamā pratipad** (Sanskrit): middle way; the **Buddha** described his teaching (***dharma***) as a middle way between self-indulgence and self-mortification, and ***paṭicca-samuppāda*** as a middle way between real existence (*atthitā*) or eternalism and complete non-existence (*n'atthitā*) or annihilationism.

manasikāra (Pali) = **manaskāra** (Sanskrit): attention, literally 'making (*kāra*) with the mind (*manas*); a characteristic of how the mind works, which can be wise (*yoniso*) or unwise (*ayoniso*); wise attention is an entrance to the spiral path.

Moggallāna (Pali) = **Maudgalyāyana** (Sanskrit): one of the **Buddha's** foremost disciples, who converted to the **Dharma** along with his friend **Sāriputta**, having heard about it in brief from **Assaji**.

moha (Pali & Sanskrit): delusion, a defiling emotion (***kilesa***) and the third of the three unskilful roots (***akusala-mūla***).

nāma (Pali & Sanskrit): name, an old Indian term used by the **Buddha** to describe how the mind works, comprising feeling (***vedanā***), perception (*saṭṭā*), intention (***cetanā***), contact (***phassa***) and attention (***manasikāra***).

nāma-rūpa (Pali & Sanskrit): name-and-form, the fourth of the twelve ***nidānas***, signifying the perceiving process and the perceived world; some versions of the ***nidāna*** chain begin with the mutual dependence of name-and-form and consciousness.

nibbāna (Pali) = **nirvāṇa** (Sanskrit): the going out of the fires of greed, hate, and delusion, the highest bliss (***sukha***) of release from ***dukkha***, the *summum bonum* of Buddhism, liberation, awakening (***bodhi***), enlightenment; nirvana is beyond words and concepts.

nibbidā (Pali) = **nirvid** (Sanskrit): disenchantment, the tenth factor (***nidāna***) of the spiral path.

nidāna (Pali & Sanskrit): link, connection, source, explanation, something which something else depends upon.

paccaya (Pali) = **pratyaya** (Sanskrit): cause or condition; ***paccaya*** is synonymous with ***hetu*** in early Buddhism but is later used to mean 'condition' as distinct from ***hetu***, meaning 'cause'.

Pali: the name given to the language in which the only complete record of the **Buddha's** teachings is preserved. In fact the word *pāli* just means 'text', and only later became the name for a language. **Pali** is probably quite similar to Māgadhī, the language spoken by the **Buddha**.

pāmojja (Pali, also *pāmujja*) = **prāmodya** (Sanskrit): joy, the third factor (***nidāna***) of the spiral path.

papañca (Pali) = **prapañca** (Sanskrit): proliferation, the psychological tendency of the mind to elaborate thoughts on the basis of feelings, and so create a world.

passaddhi (Pali) = **praśrabdhi** (Sanskrit): tranquillity, the fifth factor (***nidāna***) of the spiral path.

paṭicca-samuppāda (Pali) = **pratītya-samutpāda** (Sanskrit): dependent arising or dependent origination, the unique and distinctive teaching of the **Buddha** on conditionality. The term was invented by the **Buddha**, and consists of *paṭicca*, an absolutive meaning 'depending' or 'dependent', and *samuppāda*, an action noun mean 'arising', 'co-arising' or 'production', such that the compound ***paṭicca-samuppāda*** means 'an arising or production which is depending or dependent [on some other thing]'.

paṭicca-samuppanna (Pali) = **pratītya-samutpanna** (Sanskrit): dependently arisen, as in *paṭicca-samuppanna dhammā*, dependently arisen things.

paṭipāda majjhimā: *see* ***majjhimā paṭipadā***.

phassa (Pali) = **sparśa** (Sanskrit): contact, the sixth of the twelve ***nidānas***.

pīti (Pali) = **prīti** (Sanskrit): rapture, the fourth factor (***nidāna***) of the spiral path.

pūjā (Pali & Sanskrit): worship, an act of devotion to the **Buddha**, **Dharma**, or Sangha; traditional Buddhist ***pūjā*** involves offering flowers, candles and incense to a shrine as well as devotional chanting.

rāga (Pali & Sanskrit): greed, synonymous with ***lobha***.

rūpa (Pali & Sanskrit): form, in two senses: (1) visible form, or what is seen with the eye, as compared to sounds, odours, tastes, what is touched, and mental phenomena; and (2) physical reality in a general sense, made of the four elements, which, together with name (in ***nāma-rūpa***) arises together with consciousness (***viññāṇa***) as the third and fourth ***nidānas***.

saddhā (Pali) = **śraddhā** (Sanskrit): faith, confidence or trust, in the three jewels, the **Buddha**, the **Dharma**, and the Sangha; the second factor (***nidāna***) of the spiral path.

Sakya (Pali) = **Śākya** (Sanskrit): the name of the clan from which the **Buddha** came. The Śākyans lived in India between the Ganges river and the Himalayas, with Kapilavastu as their capital. The **Buddha** was known as *Śākyamuni* (the sage of the Śākyans) and his followers as *Śākyapūtras* (sons of the Śākyan). **Śākya** was an independent republic until it was absorbed into the Kingdom of Kosala just after the **Buddha's** death.

saḷāyatanāni (Pali) = **ṣaḍāyatanāni** (Sanskrit): the six sense realms, meaning both the sense organs and what each organ perceives; the fifth of the twelve ***nidānas***.

samādhi (Pali & Sanskrit): concentration, or meditative absorption, the seventh factor (***nidāna***) of the spiral path.

samaṇa (Pali) = **śramaṇa** (Sanskrit): ascetic, or religious renouncer, literally a 'striver'; the non-brahmanical religious wanderers of ancient India who lived on alms, and discussed philosophical and religious ideas; the **Buddha** was a ***samaṇa***, and often called 'the ***samaṇa*** Gotama'.

saṃsāra (Pali & Sanskrit): the rolling-on or cycle of rebirth according to **karma**; pictured in later Buddhism in terms of the ***bhavacakra*** or 'Wheel of Life'.

saṅkhāras (Pali) = **saṃskāras** (Sanskrit): formations, a technical term having an active meaning of 'things which construct other things', and a passive meaning of 'things that are constructed or put together'; formations in the active sense are the second of the twelve ***nidānas***, and in a passive sense are conditioned things (***saṅkhata*** *dhammas*), meaning, everything that has arisen on conditions.

saṅkhata (Pali) = **saṃskṛta** (Sanskrit): conditioned, implying having arisen on conditions.

saṃvega (Pali & Sanskrit): urgency, the mood of dismay and spiritual urgency arising from awareness of impermanence (***aniccatā***), illness, and ageing-and-death (***jarā-maraṇaṃ***).

Sanskrit: the name for the literary language of the **brahmans** of India. The word (= ***saṃskṛta***) means 'put together' and hence 'refined' as well as 'artificial'.

Sāriputta (Pali) = **Śāriputra** (Sanskrit): one of the **Buddha's** foremost disciples, who converted to the **Dharma** along with his friend **Moggallāna**, having heard about it in brief from **Assaji**.

sukha (Pali & Sanskrit): (1) pleasant, (2) bliss, the sixth factor (***nidāna***) of the spiral path.

śūnya (Sanskrit) = **suñña** (Pali): empty, used (1) by the Buddha to describe the world of experience as empty of self (***ātman***) or anything to do with self, then used (2) by Nāgārjuna and later Buddhists to denote the lack of *svabhāva* or 'intrinsic existence' in all ***dharmas***.

śūnyatā (Sanskrit) = **suññata** (Pali): emptiness, the abstract noun formed from ***śūnya***.

sutta (Pali) = **sūtra** (Sanskrit): a discourse of the **Buddha** as preserved in the *sutta-piṭaka*, the 'basket of discourses', or one of the **Mahāyāna** scriptures attributed to the **Buddha** but written centuries later.

taṇhā (Pali) = **tṛṣṇa** (Sanskrit): craving, literally 'thirst', the eighth of the twelve ***nidānas***; categorized as craving for sense-pleasures (*kāma-taṇhā*), craving for existence (***bhava***-*taṇhā*), and craving for non-existence (*vibhava-taṇhā*).

tathāgata (Pali & Sanskrit): the Realized One, literally, 'one-who-has-become-thus'; understood by later Buddhists to mean 'thus-gone' (to **nirvana**); the term is the **Buddha's** preferred way of referring to himself or to an awakened teacher.

upādāna (Pali & Sanskrit): clinging or grasping, the ninth of the twelve ***nidānas***; also means the fuel (of a fire), hence the sustenance for continued existence (***bhava***) in **samsara**.

Upaniṣads (Sanskrit): the ancient brahmanical scriptures, teaching among other things the identity of ***ātman*** and ***Brahman***. The **Buddha** might have encountered the teaching of the **Upaniṣads** indirectly, through his many discussions with **brahmans** about the nature of reality and the spiritual life.

vedanā (Pali & Sanskrit): feeling, the seventh of the twelve ***nidānas***; the hedonic response to experience, described as pleasant (***sukha***), unpleasant (***dukkha***), or neither.

vimokkha (Pali) = **vimokṣa** (Sanskrit): *see* ***vimutti***.

vimutti (Pali) = **vimukti** (Sanskrit): liberation, freedom, release, a synonym of ***bodhi***, and the eleventh factor (***nidāna***) of the spiral path.

viññāṇa (Pali) = **vijñāna** (Sanskrit): consciousness, the third of the twelve ***nidānas***; some versions of the ***nidāna*** chain begin with the mutual dependence of consciousness and name-and-form.

vipassanā (Pali) = **vipaśyanā** (Sanskrit): insight, in the sense of the breakthrough to ***yathā-bhūta-ñāṇa-dassana***.

virāga (Pali & Sanskrit): dispassion, the ninth factor (***nidāna***) of the spiral path.

yathā-bhūta-ñāṇa-dassana (Pali) = **yathā-bhūta-jñāna-darśana** (Sanskrit): knowledge and vision of reality, the insight into ***paṭicca-samuppāda*** that brings liberation; the eighth factor (***nidāna***) of the spiral path.

Notes and References

In many of these notes I give references to Pali discourses. In each case I give the names and numbers of *suttas*, or discourses, followed by a reference to volume and page number in the Pali Text Society (PTS) edition in brackets. These page numbers are usually incorporated into English translations, so they provide a useful means to find particular passages. I use the following standard abbreviations for the PTS editions:

A = *Aṅguttara Nikāya*, or 'Collection of Numbered Discourses'.
D = *Dīgha Nikāya*, or 'Collection of Long Discourses'.
Dhp = *Dhammapada*.
It = *Itivuttaka*.
M = *Majjhima Nikāya*, or 'Collection of Medium Length Discourses'.
Miln = *Milindapañha*, or 'Questions of Milinda'.
S = *Saṃyutta Nikāya*, or 'Collection of Grouped Discourses'.
Sn = *Sutta-Nipāta*.
Ud = *Udāna*.
Vin = *Vinaya Piṭaka*, or 'Basket of Discipline'.

Hence (D ii.55) is a reference to the PTS edition of the *Dīgha Nikāya*, volume 2, page 55.

For a guide to the structure and contents of the Pali canon, see the excellent introduction at www.accesstoinsight.org, under 'tipitaka'. This website also offers translations of many discourses, most by the American bhikkhu Ven. Thanissaro, and something to note is that he regularly translates *dukkha* as 'stress' and nirvana (*nibbāna*) as 'Unbinding'. Although his translation decisions are explained on the website, and have their merits, they may catch out the unwary and make the translations look more unfamiliar than they otherwise might. Other reliable print translations of the *sutta piṭaka* of the Pali canon are as follows:

Dīgha Nikāya *The Long Discourses of the Buddha* trans. Maurice Walshe, Wisdom: Boston, 1995.

Majjhima Nikāya *The Middle Length Discourses of the Buddha* trans. Bhikkhu Ñāṇamoḷi and Bhikkhu Bodhi, Wisdom: Boston, 1995.

Saṃyutta Nikāya *The Connected Discourses of the Buddha* trans. Bhikkhu Bodhi, Wisdom: Boston, 2000.

Aṅguttara Nikāya *Numerical Discourses of the Buddha* trans. Bhikkhu Bodhi and Ven. Nyanaponika, AltaMira Press 2000; NB this is an anthology of around 10% of the *Aṅguttara Nikāya*; Bhikkhu Bodhi is working on a complete translation.

Khuddhaka Nikāya The 'miscellaneous collection' includes famous works such as:

Dhammapada: the way of truth trans. Sangharakshita, Windhorse: Birmingham, 2001; trans. Buddharakkhita, 2nd ed., BPS: Kandy, 1996 (with Pali verses).

The Udāna & The Itivuttaka trans. John D. Ireland, BPS: Kandy, 1997.

The Sutta-Nipāta trans. Saddhatissa, Curzon Press: London, 1986; trans. K.R. Norman as *The Rhinoceros Horn and Other Early Buddhist Poems*, PTS: London, 1985.

Theragāthā, trans. K.R. Norman as *Poems of Early Buddhist Monks*, PTS: Oxford, 1997.

Therīgāthā, trans. K.R. Norman and C.A.F. Rhys Davids as *Poems of Early Buddhist Nuns*, PTS: Oxford, 1989.

Three excellent anthologies from the Pali scriptures are:

Sayings of the Buddha trans. Rupert Gethin, Oxford University Press, 2008.

In the Words of the Buddha trans. Bhikkhu Bodhi, Wisdom: Boston, 2005.

The Life of the Buddha trans. Bhikkhu Ñāṇamoḷi, 3rd ed., BPS: Kandy, 1992.

Introduction: Buddhism and Conditionality

1 A story very well told by Charles Allen in *The Buddha and the Sahibs: the men who discovered India's lost religion*, John Murray: London, 2002.
2 All translations from Sanskrit and Pali in this book are by the author.
3 Earlier translations of the expression *paṭicca-samuppāda* include 'conditioned co-production' (coined by Edward Conze) and 'causal genesis' (by T.W. Rhys Davids), but expressions such as 'dependent arising', 'dependent co-arising', and 'dependent origination' have now become the standard translations.
4 We use the abbreviations 'CE' ('common era') and 'BCE' ('before common era') as secular (non-Christian) alternatives to the usual AD and BC.
5 The story is found in the *Vinaya*, vol.1, pp.39–42 (Vin i.39–42).
6 William Blake, *Jerusalem*, plate 77 (entitled 'To the Christians').
7 From the 'āryapariyesanā Sutta' (Discourse on the Noble Quest), *Majjhima Nikāya*, sutta 26 (M i.163ff) (and in several other places in the Pali canon).
8 From the 'Mahānidāna Sutta' (The Great Explanation), *Dīgha Nikāya*, sutta 15 (D ii.55).
9 See Daniel Boucher, 'The *Pratītyasamutpādagāthā* and Its Role in the Medieval Cult of the Relics', *Journal of the International Association of Buddhist Studies*, 1991, vol.1, pp.1–27.
10 From the 'Vakkali Sutta' (Discourse to Vakkali), *Saṃyutta Nikāya*, 22:87 (S iii.120). The equation of the Buddha with the Dharma is also found in several other suttas.
11 This equation is found in the 'Mahāhatthipadopama Sutta' (the Greater Discourse on the Simile of the Elephant's Footprint), *Majjhima Nikāya*, sutta 28 (M i.190–1).
12 From *The Śālistamba Sūtra*, trans. N. Ross Reat, Motilal Banarsidass: Delhi, 1993, p.27.
13 This is the argument against scepticism put forward by the Buddhist scholar Richard Gombrich in *What the Buddha Thought*, Equinox: London, 2009, p.17.
14 I have put most non-English words, like *nidāna* and *dukkha*, into italics, and spelled them with the correct diacritic marks, but some words – karma, nirvana, and samsara – have become naturalized in English and so do not need any special spelling. There is a 'Pronunciation Guide for Pali and Sanskrit Words' above.

Chapter One: The Principle of Conditionality

1 From the 'Cūḷasakuludāyi Sutta' (Lesser Discourse to Sakuludāyin), *Majjhima Nikāya*, sutta 79 (M ii.32). The religious teacher mentioned is Nigaṇṭha Nātaputta, the leader of the Jains, about whom the Buddhist scriptures are mostly disparaging. Sakuludāyin, however, was unable to understand the Buddha's teaching, and even when convinced was obstructed from following it by his own followers. The discourse points to how presuppositions about the nature of spirituality can stand in the way of actual progress.

2 This formula is found in several places throughout the Pali canon in exactly the same form, for instance in the *Udāna* (Inspired Utterances), 1.1–3. The phrase *imasmiṃ sati idaṃ hoti* might more literally be rendered 'When this exists, that comes into being', and *imasmiṃ asati idaṃ na hoti* 'When this does not exist, that does not come into being'.

3 The Dharma is described as *atakkāvacara*, 'beyond the sphere of reason' or 'non-conceptual', in several places in the Pali canon, for instance in the 'āriyapariyesanā Sutta' (Discourse on the Noble Quest), *Majjima Nikāya*, sutta 26 (M i.167). Nirvana is also described as 'beyond the sphere of reason' in the *Itivuttaka*, 2.16 (PTS p.37).

4 The opening lines of 'Auguries of Innocence', from William Blake's notebooks of about 1803. I have preserved the poet's quirky Capitalization.

5 From the 'Alagaddūpama Sutta' (The Simile of the Water Snake), Majjhima Nikāya, sutta 22 (M i.140). The phrase is also found in the 'Anurādha Sutta', Saṃyutta Nikāya, 22:86 (S iii.119).

6 Here is a typical example of such an observation: 'Just as, monks, seeds that are unbroken, undecayed, unharmed by wind or heat, fresh and fertile, when sown in good soil, in well-prepared ground and supplied with seasonable rain by the gods, those seeds, monks, would thereby come to growth, increase and plenty. Just so, monks, where one's personality (*attabhāvo*) arises, there that action – done with greed [or hate, or delusion], born of greed, with greed as its condition, with greed as its origin – that action will bear fruit.' From the 'Nidāna Sutta', *Anguttara Nikāya*, 3:33 (A i.135). The image of seeds growing and bearing appropriate fruit is a common Buddhist metaphor for karma and its results.

7 The expression *paṭicca-samuppāda* is a compound consisting of *paṭicca*, an absolutive, joined to *samuppāda*, a verbal noun, and it means literally 'an arising (*samuppāda*) which is depending (*paṭicca*) [on something else]'. Compounds of this sort are unusual in Pali and Sanskrit, but not unknown, as Pali scholar K.R. Norman

shows in *The Group of Discourses*, 2nd ed., Pali Text Society: Oxford, 2001, p.175 (which is a very literal translation of the *Sutta-Nipāta*).

8 This is from the 'Cūḷamāluṅkyavāda Sutta' (The Shorter Teaching to Māluṅkya), *Majjhima Nikāya*, sutta 63 (M i.426).

9 A good introduction to the way that mindfulness can be used to help with stress is Jon Kabat-Zinn, *Full Catastrophe Living*, Piaktus: London, 1996. Mindfulness-based stress reduction courses are now widely available.

10 From 'Mahā Sakyamuni Gotamo' (Gotama the Great Sakyan Sage), *Saṃyutta Nikāya*, 12:10 (S ii.10). A 'bodhisatta' is 'someone capable of awakening', and is the term used for the Buddha prior to his awakening, equivalent to the Sanskrit 'bodhisattva'.

11 Later Buddhists developed more complex analyses of the different kinds of causes and conditions. One of the main distinctions they made was between a *hetu* (a cause) and a *paccaya* (a condition), with a *hetu* being a particular kind of *paccaya*. However, the historical Buddha does not seem to have made such fine distinctions, using the words *hetu* and *paccaya* synonymously, along with other words for cause like *samudāya*, or 'origin', and *nidāna*, or 'source'.

12 From the 'Mahāhatthipadopama Sutta' (the Greater Discourse on the Simile of the Elephant's Footprint), *Majjhima Nikāya*, sutta 28 (M i.190–1). Actually, this equation is taught by Sāriputta, who says that the Buddha had said it. Curiously, however, it does not appear anywhere else in the Pali canon.

13 The expression 'transcendental principle' for *paṭicca-samuppāda* is from Sangharakshita, *A Survey of Buddhism*, 9th ed., Windhorse: Birmingham, 2001, p.36. By the word 'transcendental' we do not mean to imply the existence of a spiritual realm above and beyond ordinary reality so much as an awakened way of knowing reality that entirely transcends the ordinary.

14 From the 'Paccaya Sutta' (Conditions), *Saṃyutta Nikāya*, 12:20 (S ii.25).

15 At this point the Buddha goes on to explain how, following the old road, he understood each of the twelve *nidānas*.

16 From the 'Nagara Sutta' (The City), *Saṃyutta Nikāya*, 12:65 (S ii.105–6).

17 From the 'Ariyapariyesanā Sutta' (Discourse on the Noble Quest), *Majjhima Nikāya*, sutta 26 (M i.167–9). The story is found in several other passages in the Pali canon too.

18 From the 'Mahānidāna Sutta' (The Great Explanation), *Dīgha Nikāya*, sutta 15 (D ii.55); the same exchange between the Buddha and Ānanda is found in the 'Nidāna Sutta', *Saṃyutta Nikāya*, 12:60 (S ii.92).

Chapter Two: The Scope of Conditionality

1 Sañjaya Belaṭṭhiputta appears as one of the six teachers who were rivals of the Buddha, apparently teaching a form of 'eel-wriggling' scepticism, according to the 'Sāmaṭṭaphala Sutta' (Discourse on the Fruits of Being a Renouncer), *Dīgha Nikāya*, sutta 2 (D i.58–9).

2 The *amataṃ* or Deathless is one of the 32 synonyms for nirvana given in the discourses of the 'Asaṅkhata Saṃyutta' (Section on the Unconditioned) in the *Saṃyutta Nikāya*, 43:12–44 (S iv.362–73). Others include *asaṅkhataṃ* (the Unconditioned), *nippapañca* (the Unproliferated), *santaṃ* (the Peaceful) and *saranaṃ* (the Refuge). Such words only gesture towards that to which they refer.

3 In Pali: *te dhammā hetuppabhavā tesaṃ hetuṃ tathāgato āha / tesañca yo nirodho evaṃvādi mahāsamaṇo.* This is slightly different from the Sanskrit version given in the Introduction.

4 The story of the conversion of Sāriputta and Moggallāna is in the *Vinaya*, vol.1, pp.39–42 (the section known as the Mahāvagga), in a long narrative recording the early history of the Sangha.

5 Sangharakshita's lecture 'Mind – Reactive and Creative' was delivered in 1967, and most recently reprinted in *Buddha Mind*, Windhorse: Birmingham, 2001. A recording of this lecture and a transcript are available on www.freebuddhistaudio.com.

6 From Sangharakshita, *Buddha Mind*, Windhorse: Birmingham, 2001, pp.38–9.

7 The term 'reactive mind' comes originally from Scientology, a controversial 20th c. psychotherapeutic movement. In Scientology, 'reactive mind' refers to unconscious mental processes consisting of accumulated impressions called 'engrams', that can be 'erased' by participation in extremely expensive 'auditing' courses. We should understand Sangharakshita to be using the term to refer to a mind and heart that, in Buddhist terms, is under the influence of the three 'unwholesome roots' of greed, hate, and delusion.

8 From Sangharakshita, *Buddha Mind*, Windhorse: Birmingham, 2001, p.53.

9 From Sangharakshita, *Buddha Mind*, Windhorse: Birmingham, 2001, pp.45–6.

10 This story is not in fact found in the 'First Sermon' but in the 'Ariyapariyesanā Sutta' (Discourse on the Noble Quest), in the *Majjhima Nikāya*, sutta 26 (M i.171–2).

11 From the 'Dhammacakkappavattana Sutta' (Discourse on the Turning of the Wheel of Dharma), at *Saṃyutta Nikāya*, 56:11 (S v.421–2). There is more of the 'First Sermon' in ch.6, on the 'middle way', below; the *khandhas* are explained in ch.7.

12 The issues involved in understanding and translating *āriya-sacca* are discussed very fully in an article by Peter Harvey, 'The Four

Ariya-saccas as True Realities for the Spiritually Ennobled – the Painful, its Origin, its Cessation, and the Way Going to This – Rather than "Noble Truths" Concerning These', in *Buddhist Studies Review*, vol.26, no.2, 2009, pp.197–227.

13 In fact, the Buddha elsewhere describes himself as a surgeon who removes the arrow of craving, having probed it with awareness; this is in the 'Sunakkhata Sutta' (Discourse to Sunakkhata), in the *Majjhima Nikāya*, sutta 105 (M ii.252).

14 From Sangharakshita, *Living with Awareness*, Windhorse: Birmingham, 2003, p.154.

15 This point is made by the Thai scholar-monk Ven. P.A. Payutto in *Dependent Origination: the Buddhist Law of Conditionality*, trans. Bruce Evans, Buddhadhamma Foundation: Bangkok, 1994, pp.106–7; also online at www.buddhanet.net/cmdsg/coarise.htm.

16 For a full discussion of the eightfold path, see Sangharakshita, *The Buddha's Noble Eightfold Path*, Windhorse: Cambridge, 2007 (a revised edition of the earlier *Vision and Transformation: an Introduction to the Buddha's Noble Eightfold Path*, Windhorse: Birmingham, 1990).

17 The ambiguities in the meaning of *taṇhā* in Buddhism, and some of the cosmic implications of transforming desire, are explored in an excellent article by Sagaramati, 'Three Cheers for Taṇhā', in *Western Buddhist Review*, vol.2, 1997; online at www.westernbuddhistreview.com.

18 From 'Mahāparinibbāna Sutta' (The Buddha's Last Days), *Dīgha Nikāya*, sutta 16 (D ii.100). The phrase 'makeshift repairs' is a translation of an obscure Pali expression, which literally means 'various straps' or possibly 'various quakings'.

19 From 'Salla Sutta' (Discourse on the Arrow), *Saṃyutta Nikāya*, 36:6 (S iv.208).

20 From 'Salla Sutta' (Discourse on the Arrow), *Saṃyutta Nikāya*, 36:6 (S iv.209).

21 For a full discussion of using awareness to work with physical pain, see Vidyamala Burch, *Living Well with Pain and Illness: The Mindful Way to Free Yourself from Suffering*, Piatkus: London, 2008.

22 *Dhammapada*, v.21. The phrase 'heedful awareness' translates *appamāda*, literally 'non-heedlessness', which could also be translated 'mindfulness' or 'vigilance'. Along with *sati* and *sampajañña*, *appamāda* is one of the main words used by the Buddha for awareness, and it particularly suggests unwavering ethical awareness.

23 From 'Māluṅkyaputta', *Saṃyutta Nikāya*, 35:95 (S iv.72). The Buddha also gave this teaching to Bāhiya, as recorded in the *Udāna* 1.10. But whereas Bāhiya was said to have immediately gained awakening upon hearing these words, Māluṅkyaputta had to go

away and work on it, and he is recorded as becoming an *arahant* at the end of the discourse.

24 Each verse is in fact repeated six times for each of the six senses. So in place of the word 'seeing' the following verses read 'hearing', then 'smelling', then 'tasting', then 'touching', then 'thinking'. These verses are also found in the *Theragāthā*, vv.794–817.

Chapter Three: The Twelve Links

1 From the *Udāna* 1.3. The *Udāna* is a collection of stories each followed by an 'inspired utterance' (*udāna*) of the Buddha (we have not included the 'inspired utterance' verses here, as they are not relevant). The same story and formula is found in the *Vinaya* 1.1. In other passages the Buddha is described as contemplating the twelve *nidānas* prior to his awakening. In the later Buddhist tradition, however, the Buddha's contemplation of the *nidāna* chain is said to have taken place on the night of his awakening, so that the twelve *nidānas* made up the intellectual content of his awakening experience. Although this is a later tradition, and not historically reliable, the story shows just how important the twelve *nidānas* were to the early Buddhists.

2 For a more detailed discussion of how several contemporary Buddhist thinkers have approached the interpretation of the twelve *nidānas* in relation to its traditional exegesis, see the article by Dhivan Thomas Jones, 'New Light on the Twelve *Nidānas*' in *Contemporary Buddhism*, vol.10 no.2, 2009, pp.241–59 (available via www.dhivan.net).

3 The symbol of the *bhavacakra* is explored in detail in Kulananda, *The Wheel of Life*, Windhorse: Birmingham, 2000.

4 The three-life interpretation of the twelve links is first recorded in the last book of the Sarvāstivādin Abhidharma, the *Jñānaprasthāna* (1st c. BCE), and then in a more developed form in the commentarial literature, in both Vasubandhu's *Abhidharmakośa* and Buddhaghosa's *Visuddhimagga*, ch.XVII (5th c. CE).

5 Fuller explanations of the traditional three-life interpretation can be found in Sangharakshita, *A Survey of Buddhism*, 9th ed., Windhorse: Birmingham, 2001, pp.128–37; and in Nyanatiloka, *Buddhist Dictionary* q.v. 'paṭiccasamuppāda' (available in many print versions, and online at www.palikanon.com/english/wtb/dic_idx.html). The Abhidharma tradition also accepted that the twelve *nidānas* could be understood as applying in strictly psychological terms to the present moment – the whole Wheel of Life going around, as it were, in a split second. In this interpretation it is the fixed sense of self – of 'I' and 'me' – that is

born and dies and is reborn throughout our lives, even from day to day and moment to moment, on condition of ignorance, craving and the rest.

6 Although we have presented *bhava* as part of the karma-process, it is usually analysed as having two aspects, as both karma-process and rebirth process. Traditionally, *bhava* is considered as karma-process inasmuch as any existence involves ignorance, formations, craving and clinging, but also as result-process, inasmuch as rebirth is the result of karma.

7 Lists of six, ten, eleven, twelve and twenty-three *nidānas* can be found among the many short suttas about *paṭicca-samuppāda* to be found in the *nidāna-saṃyutta* (all about the *nidānas*) of the *Saṃyutta Nikāya* (S ii.1–128); and nine *nidānas* are described in the 'Mahānidāna Sutta', the other *locus classicus* of the Buddha's teaching on *paṭicca-samuppāda*, in the *Dīgha Nikāya*, sutta 14 (D ii.55ff).

8 Some western Buddhists have suggested that the Buddha did not teach rebirth, but this conflicts with the evidence in the Pali scriptures. A belief in rebirth is implied throughout the canon and is often explicit, as in the 'Sāleyyaka Sutta' (Discourse to the Brahmans of Sālā), *Majjhima Nikāya*, sutta 41 (M i.285), in which the Buddha teaches rebirth in the various realms according to karma.

9 While the Buddha certainly taught rebirth, it is not necessary to believe *literally* in rebirth in order to appreciate this teaching, as it is also effective as a *metaphor* or story about the human situation. The important thing is to hold an open mind about the mystery of existence. There is a good discussion of how to approach Buddhist teachings on rebirth in Nagapriya, *Exploring Karma and Rebirth*, Windhorse: Birmingham, 2004, chs.7–12.

10 From 'Dvayatānupassanā Sutta' (Contemplation of the Pairs) in *Sutta-Nipāta*, 3:12 (Sn vv.724–65 pp.139–49). In fact, the Buddha only describes eight of the twelve *nidānas* in this discourse, without the six sense realms, existence, birth, and ageing-and-death, and he includes other factors also described as responsible for the arising of *dukkha*.

11 From the *Dhammapada*, vv.153–4. The commentary takes the house-builder to be craving, the rafters as the defilements, and the ridgepole as ignorance. The line 'mind unfabricated, open' translates *visaṅkhāragataṃ cittaṃ*, which means literally 'the mind has become without *saṅkhāras*', which are the 'formations' or tendencies that lead to the further arising of *dukkha* and to rebirth in samsara. The line has also been translated 'my heart is as one with the unmade' (Ajahn Munindo, *A Dhammapada for Contemplation*, 2nd ed., Aruna Publications, 2006, p.54) and 'the (conditioned) mind has gone to destruction' (Sangharakshita,

Dhammapada: the Way of Truth, Windhorse: Birmingham, 2001, p.58). The commentary takes this to mean the realization of nirvana.

12 Sangharakshita, *A Guide to the Buddhist Path*, 2nd ed., Windhorse: Birmingham, 1998, p.80.

13 From 'Naḷakalāpiyo Sutta' (Sheaves of Reeds), *Saṃyutta Nikāya*, 12:67 (S ii.112). The interdependence of consciousness and name-and-form is also taught in the 'Mahānidāna Sutta' (Discourse on the Great Explanation), *Dīgha Nikāya*, sutta 14 (D ii.62), and elsewhere.

14 Sangharakshita, *A Survey of Buddhism*, 9th ed., Windhorse: Birmingham, 2001, p.135.

15 To have 'the sense-gates guarded' (*indriyesu guttadvāra*) is a stage in the gradual path to *nibbāna* found in several suttas (2–13) of the *Dīgha Nikāya*. To guard the sense-gates means to live with restraint over what one allows in, such that no unwholesome reactions arise. Doing so leads to experiencing inwardly a blameless bliss.

Chapter Four: The Spiral Path

1 That *paṭicca-samuppāda* describes the whole of conditioned reality, both samsara and the path to nirvana, is one of Sangharakshita's distinctive presentations of the Dharma. The fullest account of his views on this topic is found in *A Survey of Buddhism*, 9th ed., Windhorse: Birmingham, 2001, pp.137–44. A summary can be found in Subhuti, *A New Voice in the Buddhist Tradition*, Windhorse: Birmingham, 1994, pp.65–9.

2 There is another presentation of the way to awakening that we will not examine in this book but which overlaps with the factors of the path that we will discuss. The *bojjhaṅgas*, or 'factors of awakening', are seven progressive factors commonly found in the Pali discourses: mindful awareness (*sati*), investigation of phenomena (*dhammavicaya*), energy (*viriya*), rapture (*pīti*), tranquillity (*passaddhi*), concentration (*samādhi*), and equanimity (*upekkhā*). These factors are presented as a dependently arisen series in the 'Anapanasati Sutta' (Discourse on the Mindfulness of Breathing), in *Majjhima Nikāya*, sutta 118 (M iii.85–6), and Sangharakshita discusses them in this way in 'Mind – Reactive and Creative' (*Buddha Mind*, Windhorse: Birmingham, 2001, pp.55–61).

3 This sequence of positive factors is called 'transcendental dependent arising' (*lokuttara paṭicca-samuppāda*) in the Pali commentarial work *Nettipakaraṇa*, p.67; they are discussed by Bhikkhu Bodhi in his essay 'Transcendental Dependent Arising', available online at www.accesstoinsight.org.

4 This is the 'Upanisā Sutta' (Discourse on Secret Causes), at *Saṃyutta Nikāya*, 12:23 (S ii.29). Although, following Sangharakshita, we use the term *nidānas* here in relation to these positive factors, the term *nidānas* is not in fact used of them in the Pali discourses.

5 The word *upanisā*, here translated 'basis', is understood in the commentarial tradition to be synonymous with Pali words like *paccaya, hetu,* and *nidāna*, meaning 'cause' or 'condition'. However, it is also the Pali equivalent of the Sanskrit word *upaniṣad*, which means 'hidden connection' and 'secret teaching' (as in the Upaniṣads, the Brahmanical texts that give 'secret teachings' about the *ātman*, the permanent Self, and about *Brahman*, the ultimate reality). Perhaps the Buddha was arguing with the Upaniṣads in this discourse: perhaps he was suggesting that he also has a 'secret teaching', but it is that things arise on conditions, so that ultimately there is no permanent Self to be found.

6 From Sangharakshita, *What is the Dharma?* Windhorse: Birmingham, 1998, p.105.

7 The image of the Buddhist path as a spiral is of Sangharakshita's own devising. Having the path emerge from the gap between feeling and craving is a subtle modification of the 23-fold series of conditions in the 'Upanisā Sutta', in which the Buddha taught that *dukkha* arises from birth. Sangharakshita's presentation of the whole of conditionality thus includes 24 *nidānas*, a total which does not appear in the Pali discourses as such. In the 'Appendix' I present a 24 *nidāna* reflection based on these teachings.

8 Sangharakshita, *Know Your Mind*, Windhorse: Birmingham, 1998, p.119, paraphrasing traditional formulations. In the Abhidharma tradition of psychological ethics, faith is a 'positive mental event', always present in any manifestation of the creative mind.

9 From 'Lines Composed a Few Miles Above Tintern Abbey', written in 1798. In another poem (*The Excursion*, Book IV), Wordsworth describes faith as 'a passionate intuition'.

10 In Sangharakshita, *A Survey of Buddhism*, 9th ed., Windhorse: Birmingham, 2001, p.322.

11 Just to complicate matters, the version of the 'Upanisā Sutta' preserved in Chinese translation includes the stages of ethics (*sīla*) and freedom from remorse (*avippaṭisāra*) before *dukkha* and faith (*saddhā*); see Thich Minh Châu, *The Chinese Madhyama āgama and the Pāli Majjhima nikāya: a comparative study*, 1st Indian ed., Motilal Banarsidass: Delhi, 1991, p.351. This goes to show that we should not take the discourses preserved in Pali as literally recording the exact words of the Buddha, as other scriptural traditions of equal validity preserve slightly different versions.

12 These suttas can be found in *Anguttara Nikāya*, 10:1–5 (A v.1–6).

Historically, the positive *nidāna* series beginning from ethics seems to have been the most well-known version of the spiral path, as it is also found in the *Vinaya* (Vin v.164), in Buddhaghosa's *Visuddhimagga* (p.13), and in the long 2nd c. CE poem in Sanskrit by Aśvaghoṣa called *Saundarananda*, ch.13, lines 22–6 (trans. Linda Covill, *Handsome Nanda*, New York University Press, 2007, p.247).

13 In Buddhism, shame (*hiri*, in Sanskrit, *hrī*) and fear of wrongdoing (*ottappa*, in Sanskrit, *apatrāpya*), are regarded as wholesome mental states, and indeed as *lokapālas*, or 'protectors of the world'; explored in Sangharakshita, *Know Your Mind*, Windhorse: Birmingham, 1998, pp.124–9.

14 'Confession of faults' is discussed further by Sangharakshita in *Know Your Mind*, Windhorse: Birmingham, 1998, pp.210–12.

15 This is the 'Dasuttara Sutta', from *Dīgha Nikāya*, sutta 34 (D iii.288). The entire passage reads: 'What nine states (*dhammas*) do much (*bahu-kārā*)? The nine states rooted in wise attention. From wise attention is born joy; of joy is born rapture; for one whose mind is rapturous, the body calms down (*passambhati*); someone with a calmed-down body feels bliss; the mind of someone blissful becomes concentrated; with a concentrated mind one knows and sees things just as they are (*yathārūpa*); knowing and seeing reality one is disenchanted (*nibbindati*); disenchanted, one is dispassionate (*virajjati*); and through dispassion one is liberated (*vimuccati*). These are the nine states that do much.'

16 Such wise attention is described as the quality which led the Buddha, prior to his awakening, to the discovery of each of the twelve *nidānas* responsible for *dukkha*, a discovery which led directly to full awakening: *Saṃyutta Nikāya*, 12:10 (S ii.10): 'When what exists does ageing-and-death exist? With what as condition is there ageing-and-death? Through wise attention, monks, I had the breakthrough to wisdom – when birth exists, ageing-and-death exists; with birth as condition there is ageing-and-death.' This process of discovery continues backwards through the *nidānas* until the Buddha-to-be discovers ignorance, and hence the whole arising of *dukkha*.

17 The list of five kinds of rapture comes from the later Pali commentarial tradition; see Buddhaghosa, *The Path of Purification*, trans. Ñāṇamoli, BPS: Kandy, p.141–2.

18 From Sangharakshita, *What is the Dharma?* Windhorse: Birmingham, 1998, p.115.

19 In Sangharakshita, *Know Your Mind*, Windhorse: Birmingham, 1998, p.102; this free translation draws on that by Herbert Guenther in *Mind in Buddhist Psychology*, Dharma Publishing: Berkeley, 1975, p.54.

20 From 'Cūḷadukkhakkhandha Sutta' (The Shorter Discourse on

the Mass of Suffering), in *Majjhima Nikāya*, sutta 14 (M i.94–5). Sangharakshita retells this passage as a story in *What is the Dharma?* Windhorse: Birmingham, 1998, pp.117–18.

21 This is a theme of the discourses in *Saṃyutta Nikāya*, 55, all concerned with stream-entry.

22 For instance, in 'Sāmaṭṭaphala Sutta' (Fruits of Asceticism), *Dīgha Nikāya*, sutta 2 (D i.83–4).

23 From the 'Upanisā Sutta', in the *Saṃyutta Nikāya*, 12:23 (S ii.32); the simile also occurs in *Aṅguttara Nikāya*, 10:61 and 10:62 (A v.15 & 16), in relation to a different sequence of positive factors: following the true person, listening to true Dharma, faith, wise attention, mindfulness and self-possession, sense-restraint, three good ways of practice, four applications of mindfulness, seven factors of awakening, and liberation through knowledge.

24 From a different 'Upanisā Sutta' (Discourse on Secret Causes), this one at *Aṅguttara Nikāya*, 10:3 (A v.5).

25 From *Aṅguttara Nikāya*, 10:2 (A v.4).

26 This is also from *Aṅguttara Nikāya*, 10:2 (A v.3–4), preceding the extract just quoted. The phrase 'it is not necessary to be wilful' translates the Pali expression *na cetanāya karaṇīyaṃ*, which literally means 'not to be done by *cetanā*,' where *cetanā* signifies volition or intention.

27 This comparison is in *Saṃyutta Nikāya*, 22:101 (S iii.153–4), and 'devoted to spiritual development' translates *bhāvanā-anuyogam anuyutta*, literally 'practising devotion to cultivation'.

28 From *Aṅguttara Nikāya*, 10:1 (A v.1).

Chapter Five: Karma, Conditionality and Ethics

1 *Karma* is the Sanskrit word, while *kamma* is the equivalent in Pali. We use the Sanskrit form in this book because it has become naturalized in English.

2 For the Buddha's rejection of brahmanical rituals and his replacement of them by the practice of ethics, see especially 'Cunda Sutta' (To Cunda), *Aṅguttara Nikāya*, 10:176 (A v.263), and 'Vatthūpama Sutta' (The Simile of the Cloth), *Majjhima Nikāya*, sutta 7 (M i.36).

3 Jainism is a religious movement that, like Buddhism, emerged among the *samaṇas* of ancient India. It teaches a rival path to liberation from karma and samsara, emphasizing renunciation and non-harming. See Paul Dundas, *The Jains*, 2nd ed., Routledge: Abingdon, 2002, for a recent account.

4 The Buddha's idea of karma as a response to Jain and Brahmanical ideas is discussed at length by Richard Gombrich in *What the*

Buddha Thought, Equinox: London, 2009, chs.2–4.

5 From 'Vāseṭṭha Sutta' (Discourse to Vāseṭṭha) in *Sutta-Nipāta*, 3:9 (Sn pp.122–3, vv.651–4). This discourse is also in the *Majjima Nikāya*, sutta 98.

6 From *Aṅguttara Nikāya*, 5:57 (A iii.72). This is the fifth of five topics for reflection that the Buddha recommends for everyone; the others are that one is subject to age, to disease, and to death, and will be parted from everything dear. The Buddha goes on to explain that reflecting on how one is the owner of one's actions reduces or eliminates bad conduct.

7 From the *Dhammapada*, verse 127. 'Wicked deeds' here translates *pāpa-kamma*, where *pāpa* means 'bad' rather than 'evil'. Verse 128 repeats the first three lines, and has the fourth line, 'Where death might not discover you': our deeds will catch up with us in the same way that death will inevitably find us.

8 At *Aṅguttara Nikāya*, 4:77 (A ii.80), the Buddha describes knowing the results of karma as something 'unthinkable' (*acinteyya*), and says that if one tried to work them out it would lead only to madness and distress.

9 In the 'Cūlakammavibhaṅga Sutta' (Lesser Discourse on the Analysis of Karma), *Majjhima Nikāya*, sutta 135 (M iii.202); discussed further in Nagapriya, *Exploring Karma and Rebirth*, Windhorse: Birmingham, 2004, pp.53–6.

10 In the 'Mahākammavibhaṅga Sutta' (Greater Discourse on the Analysis of Karma), *Majjhima Nikāya*, sutta 136 (M iii.207). There is a good discussion of this and the preceding sutta in Dharmacarini Manishini's article 'Kamma in Context: The Mahakammavibhangasutta and the Culakammavibhangasutta', in *Western Buddhist Review*, vol.4, published online at www.westernbuddhistreview.com.

11 From the 'Sīvaka Sutta', *Saṃyutta Nikāya*, 36:21 (S iv.230).

12 Richard Gombrich discusses this passage in *What the Buddha Thought*, Equinox: London, 2009, p.20. The three 'humours' – bile, phlegm and wind – were part of Indian medical theory of the time.

13 For instance, a well-known Tibetan Buddhist teacher had this to say about the Jews gassed during the Second World War: 'The victims were experiencing the consequences of their actions performed in previous lives. The individual victims must have done something very bad in earlier lives that led to their being treated in this way.' From an interview by Richard Hayes, *Land of No Buddha*, Windhorse: Birmingham, 1998, p.76. The later Buddhist tradition seems to have gone back to an understanding of karma influenced by Jainism.

14 These 'orders of conditionality' are adapted from the scheme of the five *niyamas* discussed in Sangharakshita, *The Three Jewels*,

Windhorse: Birmingham, 1991, pp.69–70 (originally published 1967); and *Who is the Buddha?* Windhorse: Birmingham, 1994, pp.105–8.

15 This is Buddhaghosa's explanation of how conditionality works; from *The Path of Purification*, 5th ed., trans. Bhikkhu Ñāṇamoḷi, BPS: Kandy, 1991, p.553.

16 Jain ascetics continue to starve themselves to death: see William Dalrymple, *Nine Lives: In Search of the Sacred in Modern India*, Bloomsbury: London, 2009, chapter 1, for an interview with a nun who has decided to embark on her final fast.

17 From 'Nibbedhika Sutta' (Penetrative Discourse), in *Aṅguttara Nikāya*, 6.63 (A iii.415).

18 Sangharakshita, *A Survey of Buddhism*, 9th ed., Windhorse: Birmingham, 2001, p.168.

19 From the *Dhammapada*, verses 1–2. 'Experiences' here translates *dhammas* in the sense of things that appear before the mind.

20 In one discourse the Buddha explains that if everything was due to past karma, then murderers, thieves, and so on would be murderers and thieves because of past karma, which would be to deny that they had any moral responsibility at all: *Aṇguttara Nikāya*, 3:61 (A i.173). However, because karma means intention, we are all personally responsible for what we do.

21 The story of Aṅgulimāla is recorded in *Majjhima Nikāya*, sutta 86 (M ii.97), and his verses (there are more than two) are also collected in the 'Verses of the Elders', *Therigāthā* 16:8, vv.866–91. In his interesting essay 'Who Was Aṅgulimāla?' Richard Gombrich has argued that he may have been a follower of a religious cult which taught human sacrifice as a way to salvation: *How Buddhism Began*, Athlone: London, 1996, ch.5.

22 Later Buddhist traditions categorized karmas in terms of when they ripen, what they do when they ripen, and which ones have priority. Sangharakshita presents some of these categories in a usefully simplified form in *Who Is the Buddha?* Windhorse: Birmingham, 1994, pp.108–117.

23 From *Aṅguttara Nikāya*, 3:109 (A i.263), with some repetitions simplified.

24 The classification of greed, hate, and delusion as 'defilements' is from the commentarial tradition, though the term *kilesa* often occurs in the suttas.

25 The three fires are listed at *Dīgha Nikāya*, sutta 33 (D iii.218). In the 'ādittapariyāya Sutta' (The Fire Sermon) at *Saṃyutta Nikāya*, 35:28 (S iv.19), the Buddha describes everything in the world as being on fire with the fires of greed, hate, and delusion – an image famously taken up by T.S. Eliot in his long poem, *The Wasteland*.

26 From the *Dhammapada*, v.129. The Buddha teaches a positive

version of the 'golden rule' at *Saṃyutta Nikāya*, 55:7 (S v.353–5).

27 This is the approach to Buddhist ethics taken by Sangharakshita in *The Ten Pillars of Buddhism*, 4th ed., Windhorse: Birmingham, 2004.

28 From *Dīgha Nikāya*, sutta 2 (D i.63).

29 From *Aṅguttara Nikāya*, 10:174 (A v.261–2), with repetitions simplified.

30 From the 'Kālāma Sutta', *Aṅguttara Nikāya*, 3.65 (A i.188), with repetitions simplified. 'Has love affairs' translates *paradāraṃ gacchati*, 'he goes with another's wife'.

31 For more discussion on Buddhist ethics and on the Buddhist virtues, see Damien Keown, *Buddhist Ethics: A Very Short Introduction*, Oxford University Press, 2005.

32 Aristotle, *Nichomachean Ethics*, Book II, trans. J.A.K. Thompson, rev. Hugh Tredennick, Penguin: Harmondsworth, 1976, pp.91–2.

Chapter Six: Conditionality as a Middle Way

1 This story (but not the First Sermon) is found in the 'Ariyapariyesanā Sutta' (Discourse on the Noble Quest), *Majjhima Nikāya*, sutta 26 (M i.167).

2 It is not likely that this discourse was historically the Buddha's first teaching, since it contains doctrinal formulations like the four noble truths and the eightfold path which the Buddha probably only developed later in his teaching career. Nevertheless, we can think of this sutta as the first sermon in the sense that it contains what the early Buddhists thought of as the core teachings of the Buddha. Scholars believe that some of the earliest formulations of the Buddha's teaching can be found in the *Sutta-Nipāta*, Chapters 4 and 5.

3 From the 'Dhammacakkappavattana Sutta' (Discourse on the Turning of the Wheel of Dharma), at *Saṃyutta Nikāya*, 56:11 (S v.421–2); it is also included in the 'Mahāvagga' of the *Vinaya*, 1.6.17–32 (Vin i.10–12). 'Middle way' translates *majjhimā paṭipadā*.

4 From 'Sukhamāla Sutta' (Discourse on Refinement), *Anguttara Nikāya*, 3:38 (A i.145). To this day the city of Benares is renowned for its silks.

5 From 'Mahāsaccaka Sutta' (Greater Discourse to Saccaka), *Majjhima Nikāya*, sutta 36 (M i.245–6).

6 In the 'Mahāsīhanāda Sutta' (Greater Discourse on the Lion's Roar), *Majjhima Nikāya*, sutta 12 (M i.77–82), the Buddha describes a series of extreme austerities that he performed prior to his awakening, to show that he had personal experience of their ineffectiveness.

7 From 'Kaccānagotta Sutta' (Discourse to Kaccānagotta), *Saṃyutta Nikāya*, 12:15 (S ii.17). In the Pali commentaries, 'teaching by the middle' is called a 'middle way'.

8 'Real existence' and 'complete non-existence' translate the Pali terms *atthitā* and *n'atthitā*. These are abstract nouns formed with the suffix *-tā* from the verb *atthi*, 'there is', so literally they mean 'there-is-ness' and 'there-is-not-ness'.
9 See *Upaniṣads*, trans. Patrick Olivelle, Oxford University Press, 1996, for a recent translation with a good introduction.
10 'Annihilationism', the belief that death marks the complete end of us, should be distinguished from 'nihilism', which refers to the belief (or is it more of a mood?) that existence has no ultimate meaning or purpose.
11 See 'Mahātaṇhā sankhaya Sutta' (Greater Discourse on the Destruction of Craving), *Majjhima Nikāya*, sutta 38 (M i.260).
12 From the Nicene Creed, a statement of orthodox Christian belief from 325 AD.
13 From the 'Brahmajāla Sutta' (The Net of Views), *Dīgha Nikāya*, sutta 1 (D i.17–19). In the 'Kevaddha Sutta' (To Kevaddha), *Dīgha Nikāya*, sutta 11 (D i.220–22), the Buddha tells another story in which Brahmā pompously proclaims his power while being unable to answer a question put to him by a monk.
14 Arthur Balfour, *The Foundations of Belief, being notes introductory to the study of theology*, Longmans, Green, and Co.: London, 1895, pp.30–31.

Chapter Seven: The Nature of Existence

1 The word *saṅkhāra* is notoriously difficult to translate because it has a range of specific technical meanings. We have translated it 'formations' for the sake of consistency, though exactly what this word means varies according to its context. Bhikkhu Bodhi has written a useful short essay explaining the main uses of the word *saṅkhāra* in the suttas, available at www.accesstoinsight.org/lib/authors/bodhi/bps-essay_43.html.
2 From *Dhammapada*, verse 277. 'Purity' (*visuddhi*) is a common metaphor signifying liberation.
3 From the 'Saṅkhata Sutta' (Discourse on What is Conditioned), *Aṅguttara Nikāya*, 3.47 (A i.152).
4 Han-shan, *Cold Mountain*, trans. Burton Watson, Columbia University Press: New York, 1970, p.25. The poet Han-shan, if he existed, is named after the 'cold mountain' on which he lived in the 8th or 9th c., and there are 600 poems in the collection attributed to him.
5 Sangharakshita, 'Haiku', *Collected Poems 1941/94*, Windhorse: Birmingham, 1995, p.323; reprinted in *The Heart as Origami*, ed. Padmacandra, Rising Star: London, 2005, p.36.

6 Compare this mood with, for instance, that of 'Do Not Go Gently into That Good Night' by Dylan Thomas, with its 'rage against the dying of the light'.
7 From *Therīgāthā*, verses 252, 253, 257, 261. Ambapāli has 11 stanzas altogether, all describing her aged state.
8 Thanissaro Bhikkhu describes *saṃvega* as a complex emotion made of: 'the oppressive sense of shock, dismay, and alienation that come with realizing the futility and meaninglessness of life as it is normally lived; a chastening sense of our own complacency and foolishness in having let ourselves live so blindly; and an anxious sense of urgency in trying to find a way out of the meaningless cycle.' See his 'Affirming the Truths of the Heart: the Buddhist Teachings on Samvega & Pasada', www.accesstoinsight.org/lib/authors/thanissaro/affirming.html.
9 Verses ascribed to Sakka, the chief of the gods, uttered after the passing away of the Buddha, from 'Mahāparinibbāna Sutta' (The Buddha's Last Days), *Dīgha Nikāya*, sutta 16 (D ii.157); also ascribed to the Buddha (D ii.199); and also to Moggallāna after the passing of Sāriputta, in *Theragāthā*, v.1159.
10 From *Dhammapada*, verse 278.
11 This distinction of finite world and humanity's infinite desire derives from the 19th c. philosopher Søren Kierkegaard, a founding father of existentialism, for whom this tragedy was both the source of despair and the basis of an authentic religious faith.
12 This teaching is found hidden away in the *Dīgha Nikāya*, sutta 33 (D iii.216), and also in the *Saṃyutta Nikāya*, 12:165 (S iv.56). The word *dukkhatā* is *dukkha* with the abstract suffix *-tā*, that is, 'painfulness' or 'the condition of suffering'.
13 From *Dhammapada*, verse 279.
14 'Ānanda Sutta' (Discourse to Ānanda), *Saṃyutta Nikāya*, 44:10 (S iv.400).
15 From Sanghakshita, *Know Your Mind*, Windhorse: Birmingham, 1998, p.188.
16 The scheme of the five *khandhas* occurs throughout the Pali canon, but a standard definition of them can be found at *Saṃyutta Nikāya*, 22:56 (S iii.58–61) (in the chapter or *saṃyutta* concerned with the *khandhas*).
17 From 'Vajirā Sutta', in *Saṃyutta Nikāya*, 5:10 (S i.134). The simile of a chariot and its parts was later discussed by the monk Nāgasena to illustrate the meaning of *anattā*, in the *Milindapañha* (*Questions of King Milinda*) (Miln p.25–8), a Buddhist philosophical text from around 100 BCE.
18 From 'Anattalakkhaṇa Sutta' (Discourse on the Not-Self Characteristic), *Saṃyutta Nikāya*, 22:59 (S iii.66–8); it is also included in the 'Mahāvagga' of the *Vinaya*, 1.6.38–47 (Vin i.13–

14). The Buddha elsewhere offers a third argument for *anattā*, asking whether the self is the same as, or outside, one or more of the constituents, and finding all of the various possibilities inappropriate. These three arguments are thoroughly discussed in Steven Collins, *Selfless Persons*, Cambridge University Press, 1982, pp.95–103.

19 Hence the five constituents are usually called the *pañc'upādānakkhandhā*, the 'five constituents of grasping'. The *arahant*, or awakened being, is also made up of five constituents, but is simply called *pañcakkhandhā*, because there is no more *upādāna* or grasping.

20 This is the stage of stream entry (*sotāpanna*), which involves abandoning the fetters of personality view (*sakkāya-diṭṭhi*), attachment to rites and rituals (*sīlabbata-parāmāsa*), and doubt (*vicikicchā*).

21 'Khemaka Sutta', *Saṃyutta Nikāya*, 22:89 (S ii.126–32). Khemaka was at the stage of being a 'non-returner', and the fetter of conceit (*māna*) is among the five higher fetters removed only at the stage of *arahant*-ship or full awakening.

22 From 'Akkosaka Sutta' (Discourse on Insults), *Saṃyutta Nikāya*, 7:2 (S i.161–2).

23 This topic is more fully explored in Bhikkhu Ñāṇananda, *Concept and Reality in Early Buddhist Thought*, Buddhist Publication Society: Kandy, 1971; it was Ñāṇananda who ventured 'proliferation' as a translation of *papañca*.

24 From 'Madhupiṇḍika Sutta' (The Honeyball Discourse), *Majjhima Nikāya*, sutta 18 (M i.108).

25 From 'Madhupiṇḍika Sutta' (The Honeyball Discourse), *Majjhima Nikāya*, sutta 18 (M i.111–12). The Buddha later recommended Mahākaccāna's exposition of the Dharma as being exactly as he himself would have taught it, and called it 'the honeyball discourse' because it would taste like a delicious ball of sweet rice to someone who was hungry.

26 Subhuti makes the distinction of primary and secondary experience in his talk 'Exploring the Honeyball Sutta', available on www.freebuddhistaudio.com.

27 From 'Dhatuvibhaṅga Sutta' (Analysis of the Elements), *Majjhima Nikāya*, sutta 140 (M iii.246).

28 In fact, the classification of nirvana as an 'unconditioned dhamma' is from later Buddhist scholastic thought, and is not found in the suttas. It is included here only to lead into the Buddha's own teaching concerning the *asaṅkhata*, which is more poetic and ambiguous.

29 This would be *ahetukavāda*, the teaching that things do not have a condition, a view attributed for instance to Makkhali Gosāla in the

'Sāmaṭṭaphala Sutta' (Fruits of Asceticism), *Dīgha Nikāya*, sutta 2 (D i.53).

30 This theme is explored in depth by Sangharakshita in 'Enlightenment as Experience and as Non-Experience', *The Taste of Freedom*, Windhorse: Glasgow, 1990, pp.66–93; also available on www.freebuddhistaudio.com.

31 *Saṅkhata* is the past participle of *saṅkharoti*, 'puts together', so *asaṅkhata* literally means 'not put together'. All these words, as well as *saṅkhāra*, can be derived from the Sanskrit root *kṛ*, 'make' or 'do', with the prefix *-sam*, 'together'.

32 This passage is repeated at the beginning of all the discourses on 'the unconditioned' in the 'Asaṅkhata-saṃyutta' (Chapter on the Unconditioned), *Saṃyutta Nikāya*, 43:1–12 (S iv.359–69).

33 In the discourses at *Saṃyutta Nikāya*, 43:13–44 (S iv.369–73).

34 From 'Sāmaṭṭaphala Sutta' (Fruits of Asceticism), *Dīgha Nikāya*, sutta 2 (D i.85).

35 From *Udāna*, 8:3 (Ud 80–81); also in the *Itivuttaka*, 43 (Iti 37), with some complementary verses.

36 David Hume, *A Treatise of Human Nature*, Book 1, part 4, section 6.

Chapter Eight: Emptiness and Interdependence

1 Only the Abhidharmikas of the Sarvāstivāda (the name meaning 'the theory (*vāda*) that everything (*sarva*) exists (*asti*)') took this extreme view. Abhidhammikas of the Theravāda, for instance, did not make ontological claims about their dharmas.

2 The *Prajñāpāramitā* literature is large, but the two most popular texts are in *Buddhist Wisdom: The Diamond Sutra and Heart Sutra*, trans. Edward Conze, Vintage, 2001; for a practical commentary see Sangharakshita, *Wisdom Beyond Words*, 2nd ed., Windhorse: Birmingham, 2001.

3 This translation is based on the points made by Douglas L. Berger in 'Acquiring Emptiness: Interpreting Nāgārjuna's *MMK* 24:18', *Philosophy East and West*, 60:1 (Jan 2010), pp.40–64.

4 From Nāgārjuna, *Mūlamadhyamakārikā* (Verses on the Middle Way), 24:18–19. An accessible good translation of the whole work is *The Fundamental Wisdom of the Middle Way*, trans. and comm. by Jay Garfield, Oxford University Press, 1995.

5 From Nāgārjuna, *Mūlamadhyamakārikā*, 24:11.

6 From Nāgārjuna, *Mūlamadhyamakārikā*, 24:8–9. The two levels of truth were an established part of the Abhidharma analysis, but whereas the Abhidharmikas taught that from the ultimate point of view dharmas had *svabhāva*, intrinsic existence, Nāgārjuna taught that they were ultimately empty.

7 In 'Sūññataloka Sutta' (The World is Empty), *Saṃyutta Nikāya*, 35:85, (S iv.54). The Buddha also explores emptiness in the 'Cūḷasuññata Sutta' (Lesser Discourse on Emptiness) and 'Mahāsuññata Sutta' (Greater Discourse on Emptiness), *Majjhima Nikāya*, suttas 121 & 122 (M iii.104 & 109).

8 In 'Pheṇapiṇḍūpama Sutta' (The Simile of a Ball of Foam), *Saṃyutta Nikāya*, 22:95 (S iii.140).

9 In Herbert V. Guenther, *The Tantric View of Life*, Shambhala: Boulder & London, 1975, p.150.

10 Hua-yen Buddhism is explored more thoroughly in Paul Williams, *Mahāyāna Buddhism*, Routledge: Abingdon, 1989, ch.6.

11 Summarized in Sangharakshita, *The Eternal Legacy*, Windhorse: Birmingham, 2006, pp.212–14 (originally published 1985).

12 From Francis H. Cook, *Hua-yen Buddhism: the Jewel Net of Indra*, Pennsylvania State University, 1977, p.2.

13 For instance, see David Brazier, *The New Buddhism*, Constable: London, 2001, pp.102–6.

14 From Alexander Pope, *An Essay on Man*, Epistle 3, ll.7–26.

15 From Samuel Taylor Coleridge, 'The Eolian Harp', ll.26–33; these lines were added in 1817 to the original 'conversation poem' of 1795.

16 The influence of Romanticism on the reception of *paṭicca-samuppāda* in the west is explored more fully in David L. McMahan, *The Making of Buddhist Modernism*, Oxford University Press, 2008, Chapter 6, 'A Brief History of Interdependence'. Thanissaro Bhikkhu explores the same theme in a critical and practice-oriented way in his 1999 essay 'The Roots of Buddhist Romanticism', available on www.dhammatalks.org in the Essay Book 'Purity of Heart'.

17 Sangharakshita, *What is the Dharma?* Windhorse: Birmingham, 1998, pp.164–5.

18 The Vietnamese Buddhist teacher Thich Nhat Hanh has coined the term 'interbeing' to describe the mode of existence of interdependent things: see for instance Thich Nhat Hanh, *The Heart of the Buddha's Teaching*, Rider: London, 1998, ch.27, pp.221–49.

19 Her ideas are found in full in Joanna Macy, *Mutual Causality in Buddhism and General Systems Theory*, State University of New York Press: Albany, 1991, and in a more accessible short version in Joanna Macy, *World as Lover, World as Self*, Rider: London, 1993, part 2.

20 Joanna Macy, *Mutual Causality in Buddhism and General Systems Theory*, State University of New York Press: Albany, 1991, p.14.

21 See, for instance, ch. 18 on 'Interpenetration' in Fritjof Capra, *The Tao of Physics*, HarperCollins: London, 1991 (originally published 1975).

22 A theme explored in Richard Layard, *Happiness: lessons from a new science*, Penguin: London, 2005.
23 Macy uses the somewhat self-contradictory term 'mutual causality' instead of 'interdependence'.
24 For instance, in 'Naḷakalāpiyo Sutta' (Sheaves of Reeds), *Saṃyutta Nikāya*, 12:67 (S ii.112), and in the 'Mahānidāna Sutta' (Discourse on the Great Explanation), *Dīgha Nikāya*, sutta 14 (D ii.62).
25 From 'Dukkha Sutta' (Discourse on Suffering), *Saṃyutta Nikāya*, 12:43 (S ii.72), but found elsewhere too.

Appendix: 24 Nidāna Reflection

1 An audio version of the '24 *Nidāna* Reflection' is available on www.freebuddhistaudio.com under 'meditation'.
2 The version devised by Sangharakshita is described in full in Kamalashila, *Meditation: the Buddhist way of tranquillity and insight*, 2nd ed., Windhorse: Birmingham, 1996, pp.217–24. Kamalashila's book also contains general guidance on reflection practice.
3 The three levels of understanding are listed in the 'Sangīti Sutta', *Dīgha Nikāya*, sutta 33; and explored in more detail in Kamalashila, *Meditation: the Buddhist way of tranquillity and insight*, 2nd ed., Windhorse: Birmingham, 1996, pp.181–7.

Pronunciation Guide for Pali and Sanskrit Words

1 Based on Andrew Skilton, *A Concise History of Buddhism*, Windhorse: Birmingham, 1994, p.4.

Index

Buddha (*cont.*)
not different from Dharma 9–10
on pain 47–8
on proliferation 140
on sage at peace 142
on self-mortification 116
on skilful and unsilful action 106, 108–9
Song of Victory 63–4
as source for scriptures 11
on unconditioned 143, 144
on twelve links 53–4
Buddhaghosa 102
burial mound *(stūpa)* 6, 9

C

causality 27, 156–7, 160
cessation 46–9, 75, 119
chaos theory 158
character 108
characteristics of existence 87, 126–138
city, ancient (simile) 30
clinging 59, 60, 72, 167–8
Coleridge, Samuel T. 155
concentration 86–7, 165
consciousness 23, 122, 124
as constituent 134
as link 58–68, 166–7
see also: constituents, five
conditionality (see also: dependent arising)
applications of 17
and Buddhism 5–12
and causation 27
core teachings 16–33
conditionality (*cont.*)
and emptiness 146–151
and ethics 98–100
and evolution 124
formula 17
and four noble truths 43
and interdependence 156–161
and karma 96–110
as middle way 112–24
Nagarjuna on 148
orders of 101–2
principle of 16–33
on right view 119
scope of 35–52
spiral mode 77–8
as transcendental principle 28–31
confession 83
conflict 138–42
consciousness 58, 60, 66–7
and brain 114
see also: constituents, five
constituents, five *(khandas)* 134–7, 148, 150
consumerism 124
contact 59, 60, 69, 167
Contemplation of the Pairs 62
conventional truth
see: truth, two levels of
Cook, Francis 152
craving 60, 70, 167
for annihilation 45
and *dukkha* in four noble truths 44–6
creative mind
see: mind, creative

D

Daṇḍapāni 140
death 27
see also: old-age-and-death
Deathless, the 38, 49, 63, 142
Deer Park 43, 112–13, 135
defilements 56, 107
demon *(asura)* 56
delusion
see: ignorance
see also: defilements; roots, three
dependent arising
is the Dharma 9–10, 29
difficult 8–9
verses 5–8
desire
for sensual pleasure 47
for truth 47
determinism 105, 112
deva
see: god
devotion 81
Dhammapada 104, 127
Dharma
as difficult 31–3
etymology 29
as practical teaching 20–3
same as dependent arising 29
dharmadhātu (realm of reality) 153
dharmas ('things') 147–8
disenchantment 88, 168–9
disgust 45, 115
dispassion 88, 137, 169
dukkha 19, 20
(see also: stress)
cause of 28
and craving 44–6
defn. 21
end of 50
as first stage of spiral path 78–9, 164
and links 61–4
as 'mark' of existence 127–131

Romantics 154–5
roots, three (greed, hate, delusion)
skilful 107
unskilful or unwholesome 65, 107
rūpa (form)
see: constituents, five

S

sacred places 5
sage at peace 142
Sakuladayin 16
Śālistamba Sutra 10
samādhi
see: concentration; meditation
samaṇa 35
Sangharakshita
on causality 156
on craving 45–6
on creative mind 41–2
on ego 133–4
on ethics of intention 103
on 'the gap' 70
haiku 128
and 'higher hedonism' 115
on ignorance (*avidya*) 65
on interdependence 156
on mind reactive and creative 39
on no self 156
on rapture 85
on spiral condtionality 77
on tranquility 85
sankhāras (formations)
see: constituents, five
Sāriputta 6, 36–8, 67
Śāriputra (Skt)
see Sāriputta
Sarnath 43
Sañjaya 36
saññā
see: constituents, five
science 20, 157–8
scientific materialism 123–4
seals, clay 5
Self (*ātman*) 22, 67, 72
after death 121–2
see also: no self
self-mortification 113, 114–18
sense realms or spheres, six 56–60, 68–9, 167
shame 83
Sīvaka 100
skilful and unskillful
defn. 99
see also: action, roots
spiral path 75–94
approach to 92–4
factors of 75–8
images for 90–91
reflections 164–6
Spirit of Life 42
śramaṇa (Skt)
see *samana*
stream entry 88
stress 23–6, 120, 158–60
stūpa
see: burial mound
śūnyatā
see: emptiness
systems theory 157–60

T

Taoism 153
theism 122
thirst 59
see also: craving
'Tintern Abbey' 81
tranquility 85, 165
tree
bodhi 53–4
goatherd's banyan 32
as image for path 18, 91
truths, four noble
see: four noble truths
truth, two levels of 149

U

unconditioned, the 143–5
see also: nirvana; enlightenment
understanding, three levels of 169–70
unsatisfactoriness see *dukkha*
Upāli 98
Upanisā Sutta 76, 82
Upaniṣads 21, 122, 131
urgency 129

V

Vacchagotta 131, 149
Vairocana's tower 152
Vajirā 134–5
Vakkhali 9
vedana
see: feeling
Victory, Song of 63–4
viññaṇā
see: consciousness
vinaya 98

W

water image 90
Wheel of Life 40
and three-lives 56–61
wilfulness 93, 116
wisdom 64
see also: insight
wise attention 26, 83–4
see also 'awareness'
Wordsworth, William 81, 153

Y

Yama 56

Windhorse Publications is a Buddhist publishing house, staffed by practising Buddhists. We place great emphasis on producing books of high quality which are accessible and relevant to those interested in Buddhism at whatever level. Drawing on the whole range of the Buddhist tradition, our books include translations of traditional texts, commentaries, books that make links with Western culture and ways of life, biographies of Buddhists, and works on meditation.

As a charitable institution we welcome donations to help us continue our work. We also welcome manuscripts on aspects of Buddhism or meditation. To join our mailing list, place an order, or request a catalogue please visit our website at www.windhorsepublications.com or contact:

Windhorse Publications Ltd.	Perseus Distribution	Windhorse Books
169 Mill Road	1094 Flex Drive	PO Box 574
Cambridge CB1 3AN	Jackson TN 38301	Newtown NSW 2042
UK	USA	Australia

Windhorse Publications is an arm of the Triratna Buddhist Community, which has more than sixty centres on five continents. Through these centres, members of the Triratna Buddhist Community offer regular programmes of events for the general public and for more experienced students. These include meditation classes, public talks, study on Buddhist themes and texts, and bodywork classes such as t'ai chi, yoga, and massage. Triratna also run several retreat centres and the Karuna Trust, a fundraising charity that supports social welfare projects in the slums and villages of Southern Asia.

Many Triratna centres have residential spiritual communities and ethical businesses associated with them. Arts activities are encouraged too, as is the development of strong bonds of friendship between people who share the same ideals. In this way Triratna is developing a unique approach to Buddhism, not simply as a set of techniques, but as a creatively directed way of life.

If you would like more information about Triratna please visit www.thebuddhistcentre.org or write to:

London Buddhist Centre	Aryaloka	Sydney Buddhist Centre
51 Roman Road	14 Heartwood Circle	24 Enmore Road
London E2 0HU	Newmarket NH 03857	Sydney NSW 2042
UK	USA	Australia